Travel phrasebooks collection
«Everything Will Be Okay!»

CW00522203

PHRASEBOOK
– UKRAINIAN –

By Andrey Taranov

THE MOST IMPORTANT PHRASES

This phrasebook contains
the most important
phrases and questions
for basic communication
Everything you need
to survive overseas

T&P BOOKS

Phrasebook + 3000-word dictionary

English-Ukrainian phrasebook & topical vocabulary

By Andrey Taranov

The collection of "Everything Will Be Okay" travel phrasebooks published by T&P Books is designed for people traveling abroad for tourism and business. The phrasebooks contain what matters most - the essentials for basic communication. This is an indispensable set of phrases to "survive" while abroad.

This book also includes a small topical vocabulary that contains roughly 3,000 of the most frequently used words. Another section of the phrasebook provides a gastronomical dictionary that may help you order food at a restaurant or buy groceries at the store.

T&P Books Publishing
www.tpbooks.com

ISBN: 978-1-78616-763-7

This book is also available in E-book formats.
Please visit www.tpbooks.com or the major online bookstores.

FOREWORD

The collection of "Everything Will Be Okay" travel phrasebooks published by T&P Books is designed for people traveling abroad for tourism and business. The phrasebooks contain what matters most - the essentials for basic communication. This is an indispensable set of phrases to "survive" while abroad.

This phrasebook will help you in most cases where you need to ask something, get directions, find out how much something costs, etc. It can also resolve difficult communication situations where gestures just won't help.

This book contains a lot of phrases that have been grouped according to the most relevant topics. The edition also includes a small vocabulary that contains roughly 3,000 of the most frequently used words. Another section of the phrasebook provides a gastronomical dictionary that may help you order food at a restaurant or buy groceries at the store.

Take "Everything Will Be Okay" phrasebook with you on the road and you'll have an irreplaceable traveling companion who will help you find your way out of any situation and teach you to not fear speaking with foreigners.

TABLE OF CONTENTS

T&P Books Publishing

PRONUNCIATION

Letter	Ukrainian example	T&P phonetic alphabet	English example

Vowels

А а	акт	[a]	shorter than in ask
Е е	берет	[e], [ɛ]	absent, pet
Є є	модельєр	[ɛ]	man, bad
И и	ритм	[k]	clock, kiss
I i	компанія	[i]	shorter than in feet
Ї ї	поїзд	[ji]	playing, spying
О о	око	[ɔ]	bottle, doctor
У у	буря	[u]	book
Ю ю	костюм	[ˈu]	cued, cute
Я я	маяк	[ja], [ˈa]	royal

Consonants

Б б	бездна	[b]	baby, book
В в	вікно	[w]	vase, winter
Г г	готель	[ɦ]	between [g] and [h]
Ґ ґ	ґудзик	[g]	game, gold
Д д	дефіс	[d]	day, doctor
Ж ж	жанр	[ʒ]	forge, pleasure
З з	зброя	[z]	zebra, please
Й й	йти	[j]	yes, New York
К к	крок	[k]	clock, kiss
Л л	лев	[l]	lace, people
М м	мати	[m]	magic, milk
Н н	назва	[n]	name, normal
П п	приз	[p]	pencil, private
Р р	радість	[r]	rice, radio
С с	сон	[s]	city, boss
Т т	тир	[t]	tourist, trip
Ф ф	фарба	[f]	face, food
Х х	холод	[h]	home, have
Ц ц	церква	[ts]	cats, tsetse fly
Ч ч	час	[tʃ]	church, French

Letter	Ukrainian example	T&P phonetic alphabet	English example
Ш ш	шуба	[ʃ]	machine, shark
Щ щ	щука	[ɕ]	sheep, shop
ь	камінь	[ʲ]	soft sign - no sound
ъ	ім'я	[ˈ]	hard sign, no sound

LIST OF ABBREVIATIONS

English abbreviations

ab.	-	about
adj	-	adjective
adv	-	adverb
anim.	-	animate
as adj	-	attributive noun used as adjective
e.g.	-	for example
etc.	-	et cetera
fam.	-	familiar
fem.	-	feminine
form.	-	formal
inanim.	-	inanimate
masc.	-	masculine
math	-	mathematics
mil.	-	military
n	-	noun
pl	-	plural
pron.	-	pronoun
sb	-	somebody
sing.	-	singular
sth	-	something
v aux	-	auxiliary verb
vi	-	intransitive verb
vi, vt	-	intransitive, transitive verb
vt	-	transitive verb

Ukrainian abbreviations

ж	-	feminine noun
мн	-	plural
с	-	neuter
ч	-	masculine noun

UKRAINIAN PHRASEBOOK

This section contains important phrases that may come in handy in various real-life situations.
The phrasebook will help you ask for directions, clarify a price, buy tickets, and order food at a restaurant

T&P Books Publishing

PHRASEBOOK
CONTENTS

T&P Books Publishing

The bare minimum

Excuse me, ...

Вибачте, ...
['wɨbatʃtɛ, ...]

Hello.

Добрий день.
['dɔbrɨj dɛnʲ.]

Thank you.

Дякую.
['dʲakuʲu.]

Good bye.

До побачення.
[do po'batʃɛnʲa.]

Yes.

Так.
[tak.]

No.

Ні.
[ni.]

I don't know.

Я не знаю.
[ja nɛ 'znaʲu.]

Where? | Where to? | When?

Де? | Куди? | Коли?
[dɛ? | ku'dɨ? | ko'lɨ?]

I need ...

Мені потрібен ...
[mɛ'ni po'tribɛn ...]

I want ...

Я хочу ...
[ja 'hɔtʃu ...]

Do you have ...?

У вас є ...?
[u was 'ɛ ...?]

Is there a ... here?

Тут є ...?
[tut ɛ ...?]

May I ...?

Чи можна мені ...?
[tʃɨ 'mɔʒna mɛ'ni ...?]

..., please (polite request)

Будь ласка
[budʲ 'laska]

I'm looking for ...

Я шукаю ...
[ja ʃu'kaʲu ...]

restroom

туалет
[tua'lɛt]

ATM

банкомат
[banko'mat]

pharmacy (drugstore)

аптеку
[ap'tɛku]

hospital

лікарню
[li'karnʲu]

police station

поліцейську дільницю
[poli'tsɛjsʲku dilʲʲnɨtsʲu]

subway

метро
[mɛt'rɔ]

taxi	**таксі** [tak'si]
train station	**вокзал** [wok'zal]

My name is …	**Мене звуть …** [mɛ'nɛ zwutʲ …]
What's your name?	**Як вас звуть?** [jak was 'zwutʲ?]
Could you please help me?	**Допоможіть мені, будь ласка.** [dopomo'ʒitʲ mɛ'ni, budʲ 'laska.]
I've got a problem.	**У мене проблема.** [u 'mɛnɛ prob'lɛma.]
I don't feel well.	**Мені погано.** [mɛ'ni po'ɦano.]
Call an ambulance!	**Викличте швидку!** ['wiklitʃtɛ ʃwid'ku!]
May I make a call?	**Чи можна мені зателефонувати?** [tʃi 'moʒna mɛ'ni zatɛlɛfonu'wati?]

I'm sorry.	**Прошу вибачення** ['proʃu 'wibatʃɛnʲa]
You're welcome.	**Прошу** ['proʃu]

I, me	**я** [ja]
you (inform.)	**ти** [ti]
he	**він** [win]
she	**вона** [wo'na]
they (masc.)	**вони** [wo'nɨ]
they (fem.)	**вони** [wo'nɨ]
we	**ми** [mɨ]
you (pl)	**ви** [wɨ]
you (sg, form.)	**Ви** [wɨ]

ENTRANCE	**ВХІД** [whid]
EXIT	**ВИХІД** ['wihid]
OUT OF ORDER	**НЕ ПРАЦЮЄ** [nɛ pra'tsʲuɛ]
CLOSED	**ЗАКРИТО** [za'krito]

OPEN	**ВІДКРИТО** [wid'krito]
FOR WOMEN	**ДЛЯ ЖІНОК** [dlʲa ʒi'nɔk]
FOR MEN	**ДЛЯ ЧОЛОВІКІВ** [dlʲa ʧolowi'kiw]

Questions

Where?	**Де?** [dɛ?]
Where to?	**Куди?** [ku'dɨ?]
Where from?	**Звідки?** ['zwidkɨ?]
Why?	**Чому?** [ʧo'mu?]
For what reason?	**Навіщо?** [na'wiɕo?]
When?	**Коли?** [ko'lɨ?]

How long?	**Скільки часу?** ['skilʲkɨ 'ʧasu?]
At what time?	**О котрій?** [o kot'rij?]
How much?	**Скільки коштує?** ['skilʲkɨ 'kɔʃtuɛ?]
Do you have ...?	**У вас є ...?** [u was 'ɛ ...?]
Where is ...?	**Де знаходиться ...?** [dɛ zna'hɔdɨtʲsʲa ...?]

What time is it?	**Котра година?** [ko'tra ɦo'dɨna?]
May I make a call?	**Чи можна мені зателефонувати?** [ʧɨ 'mɔʒna mɛ'ni zatɛlɛfonu'watɨ?]
Who's there?	**Хто там?** [hto tam?]
Can I smoke here?	**Чи можна мені тут палити?** [ʧɨ 'mɔʒna mɛ'ni tut pa'lɨtɨ?]
May I ...?	**Чи можна мені ...?** [ʧɨ 'mɔʒna mɛ'ni ...?]

Needs

I'd like …	**Я б хотів /хотіла/ …** [ja b ho'tiw /ho'tila/ …]
I don't want …	**Я не хочу …** [ja nɛ 'hɔtʃu …]
I'm thirsty.	**Я хочу пити.** [ja 'hɔtʃu 'pitɨ.]
I want to sleep.	**Я хочу спати.** [ja 'hɔtʃu 'spatɨ.]

I want …	**Я хочу …** [ja 'hɔtʃu …]
to wash up	**вмитися** ['wmitisʲa]
to brush my teeth	**почистити зуби** [po'tʃistitɨ 'zubɨ]
to rest a while	**трохи відпочити** ['trɔhɨ widpo'tʃiti]
to change my clothes	**переодягнутися** [pɛrɛodʲahˈnutisʲa]

to go back to the hotel	**повернутися в готель** [powɛr'nutisʲa w ɦo'tɛlʲ]
to buy …	**купити …** [ku'pitɨ …]
to go to …	**з'їздити в …** ['zʲʔizdɨtɨ w …]
to visit …	**відвідати …** [wid'widatɨ …]
to meet with …	**зустрітися з …** [zust'ritisʲa z …]
to make a call	**зателефонувати** [zatɛlɛfonu'watɨ]

I'm tired.	**Я втомився /втомилася/.** [ja wto'miwsʲa /wto'milasʲa/.]
We are tired.	**Ми втомилися.** [mɨ wto'milɨsʲa.]
I'm cold.	**Мені холодно.** [mɛ'ni 'hɔlodno.]
I'm hot.	**Мені спекотно.** [mɛ'ni spɛ'kɔtno.]
I'm OK.	**Мені нормально.** [mɛ'ni nor'malʲno.]

I need to make a call. **Мені треба зателефонувати.**
[mɛ'ni 'trɛba zatɛlɛfonu'wati.]

I need to go to the restroom. **Мені треба в туалет.**
[mɛ'ni 'trɛba w tua'lɛt.]

I have to go. **Мені вже час.**
[mɛ'ni wʒɛ tʃas.]

I have to go now. **Мушу вже йти.**
['muʃu wʒɛ jti.]

Asking for directions

Excuse me, ...

Вибачте, ...
['wɨbatʃtɛ, ...]

Where is ...?

Де знаходиться ...?
[dɛ zna'hɔdɨtʲsʲa ...?]

Which way is ...?

В якому напрямку знаходиться ...?
[w ja'kɔmu 'naprʲamku zna'hɔdɨtʲsʲa ...?]

Could you help me, please?

Допоможіть мені, будь ласка.
[dopomo'ʒɨtʲ mɛ'ni, budʲ 'laska.]

I'm looking for ...

Я шукаю ...
[ja ʃu'kaʲu ...]

I'm looking for the exit.

Я шукаю вихід.
[ja ʃu'kaʲu 'wɨhid.]

I'm going to ...

Я їду в ...
[ja 'idu w ...]

Am I going the right way to ...?

Чи правильно я йду ...?
[tʃɨ 'prawɨlʲno ja jdu ...?]

Is it far?

Це далеко?
[tsɛ da'lɛkɔ?]

Can I get there on foot?

Чи дійду я туди пішки?
[tʃɨ dij'du ja tu'dɨ 'piʃkɨ?]

Can you show me on the map?

Покажіть мені на карті, будь ласка.
[poka'ʒɨtʲ mɛ'ni na 'karti, budʲ 'laska.]

Show me where we are right now.

Покажіть, де ми зараз.
[poka'ʒɨtʲ, dɛ mɨ 'zaraz.]

Here

Тут
[tut]

There

Там
[tam]

This way

Сюди
[sʲu'dɨ]

Turn right.

Поверніть направо.
[powɛr'nitʲ na'prawo.]

Turn left.

Поверніть наліво.
[powɛr'nitʲ na'liwo.]

first (second, third) turn

перший (другий, третій) поворот
['pɛrʃɨj ('druhɨj, 'trɛtij) powo'rɔt]

to the right

направо
[na'prawo]

to the left

налiво
[na'liwo]

Go straight ahead.

Iдiть прямо.
[i'dit^j 'pr^jamo.]

Signs

WELCOME!	**ЛАСКАВО ПРОСИМО** [las'kawo 'prɔsimo]
ENTRANCE	**ВХІД** [whid]
EXIT	**ВИХІД** ['wihid]

PUSH	**ВІД СЕБЕ** [wid 'sɛbɛ]
PULL	**ДО СЕБЕ** [do 'sɛbɛ]
OPEN	**ВІДКРИТО** [wid'krito]
CLOSED	**ЗАКРИТО** [za'krito]

FOR WOMEN	**ДЛЯ ЖІНОК** [dlʲa ʒi'nɔk]
FOR MEN	**ДЛЯ ЧОЛОВІКІВ** [dlʲa tʃolowi'kiw]
GENTLEMEN, GENTS (m)	**ЧОЛОВІЧИЙ ТУАЛЕТ** [tʃolo'witʃij tua'lɛt]
WOMEN (f)	**ЖІНОЧИЙ ТУАЛЕТ** [ʒi'nɔtʃij tua'lɛt]

DISCOUNTS	**ЗНИЖКИ** ['znɨʒki]
SALE	**РОЗПРОДАЖ** [roz'prɔdaʒ]
FREE	**БЕЗКОШТОВНО** [bɛzkoʃ'tɔwno]
NEW!	**НОВИНКА!** [no'winka!]
ATTENTION!	**УВАГА!** [u'waɦa!]

NO VACANCIES	**МІСЦЬ НЕМАЄ** [mists nɛ'maɛ]
RESERVED	**ЗАРЕЗЕРВОВАНО** [zarɛzɛr'wɔwano]
ADMINISTRATION	**АДМІНІСТРАЦІЯ** [admini'stratsiʲa]
STAFF ONLY	**ТІЛЬКИ ДЛЯ ПЕРСОНАЛУ** ['tilʲki dlʲa pɛrso'nalu]

BEWARE OF THE DOG!	**ЗЛИЙ СОБАКА** [złij so'baka]
NO SMOKING!	**НЕ ПАЛИТИ!** [nɛ pa'łiti!]
DO NOT TOUCH!	**РУКАМИ НЕ ТОРКАТИСЯ!** [ru'kamɨ nɛ tor'katisʲa!]
DANGEROUS	**НЕБЕЗПЕЧНО** [nɛbɛz'pɛʧno]
DANGER	**НЕБЕЗПЕКА** [nɛbɛz'pɛka]
HIGH VOLTAGE	**ВИСОКА НАПРУГА** [wɨ'soka na'pruɦa]
NO SWIMMING!	**КУПАТИСЯ ЗАБОРОНЕНО** [ku'patisʲa zabo'rɔnɛno]

OUT OF ORDER	**НЕ ПРАЦЮЄ** [nɛ pra'ʦʲuɛ]
FLAMMABLE	**ВОГНЕНЕБЕЗПЕЧНО** ['woɦnɛ nɛbɛz'pɛʧno]
FORBIDDEN	**ЗАБОРОНЕНО** [zabo'rɔnɛno]
NO TRESPASSING!	**ПРОХІД ЗАБОРОНЕНИЙ** [pro'hid zabo'rɔnɛnɨj]
WET PAINT	**ПОФАРБОВАНО** [pofar'bɔwano]

CLOSED FOR RENOVATIONS	**ЗАКРИТО НА РЕМОНТ** [za'krɨto na rɛ'mɔnt]
WORKS AHEAD	**РЕМОНТНІ РОБОТИ** [rɛ'mɔntni ro'bɔtɨ]
DETOUR	**ОБ'ЇЗД** [ob"izd]

Transportation. General phrases

plane	**літак** [li'tak]
train	**поїзд** ['pɔizd]
bus	**автобус** [aw'tɔbus]
ferry	**пором** [po'rɔm]
taxi	**таксі** [tak'si]
car	**автомобіль** [awtomo'bilʲ]

schedule	**розклад** ['rɔzklad]
Where can I see the schedule?	**Де можна подивитися розклад?** [dɛ 'mɔʒna podiʲwitisʲa 'rɔzklad?]
workdays (weekdays)	**робочі дні** [ro'bɔtʃi dni]
weekends	**вихідні дні** [wihid'ni dni]
holidays	**святкові дні** [swʲat'kɔwi dni]

DEPARTURE	**ВІДПРАВЛЕННЯ** [wid'prawlɛnʲa]
ARRIVAL	**ПРИБУТТЯ** [pribut'tʲa]
DELAYED	**ЗАТРИМУЄТЬСЯ** [za'trimuɛtʲsʲa]
CANCELLED	**ВІДМІНЕНИЙ** [wid'minɛnij]

next (train, etc.)	**наступний** [na'stupnij]
first	**перший** ['pɛrʃij]
last	**останній** [os'tanij]

When is the next ...?	**Коли буде наступний ...?** [ko'łi 'budɛ na'stupnij ...?]
When is the first ...?	**Коли відправляється перший ...?** [ko'łi widpraw'lʲaɛtʲsʲa 'pɛrʃij ...?]

When is the last ...?
Коли відправляється останній ...?
[ko'li widpraw'lʲaɛtʲsʲa os'tanij ...?]

transfer (change of trains, etc.)
пересадка
[pɛrɛ'sadka]

to make a transfer
зробити пересадку
[zro'bɨtɨ pɛrɛ'sadku]

Do I need to make a transfer?
Чи потрібно мені робити пересадку?
[tʃɨ pot'ribno mɛ'ni ro'bɨtɨ pɛrɛ'sadku?]

Buying tickets

Where can I buy tickets?	**Де я можу купити квитки?** [dɛ ja 'mɔʒu ku'pitɨ kwɨt'kɨ?]
ticket	**квиток** [kwɨ'tɔk]
to buy a ticket	**купити квиток** [ku'pitɨ kwɨ'tɔk]
ticket price	**вартість квитка** ['wartistʲ kwɨt'ka]
Where to?	**Куди?** [ku'dɨ?]
To what station?	**До якої станції?** [do ja'kɔi 'stantsii?]
I need …	**Мені потрібно …** [mɛ'ni po'tribno …]
one ticket	**один квиток** [o'dɨn kwɨ'tɔk]
two tickets	**два квитки** [dwa kwɨt'kɨ]
three tickets	**три квитки** [trɨ kwɨt'kɨ]
one-way	**в один кінець** [w o'dɨn ki'nɛts]
round-trip	**туди і назад** [tu'dɨ i na'zad]
first class	**перший клас** ['pɛrʃɨj klas]
second class	**другий клас** ['druɦɨj klas]
today	**сьогодні** [sʲo'ɦodni]
tomorrow	**завтра** ['zawtra]
the day after tomorrow	**післязавтра** [pislʲa'zawtra]
in the morning	**вранці** ['wrantsi]
in the afternoon	**вдень** ['wdɛnʲ]
in the evening	**ввечері** ['wvɛtʃɛri]

aisle seat

місце біля проходу
['mistsɛ 'biʎa pro'hɔdu]

window seat

місце біля вікна
['mistsɛ 'biʎa wik'na]

How much?

Скільки?
['skiʎkɨ?]

Can I pay by credit card?

Чи можу я заплатити карткою?
[tʃɨ 'mɔʒu ja zapla'tɨtɨ 'kartkɔʲu?]

Bus

bus	**автобус** [aw'tɔbus]
intercity bus	**міжміський автобус** [miʒmisʲˈkij aw'tɔbus]
bus stop	**автобусна зупинка** [aw'tɔbusna zu'pinka]
Where's the nearest bus stop?	**Де найближча автобусна зупинка?** [dɛ najbˈliʒtʃa aw'tɔbusna zu'pinka?]

number (bus ~, etc.)	**номер** ['nɔmɛr]
Which bus do I take to get to …?	**Який автобус їде до …?** [ja'kij aw'tɔbus 'idɛ do …?]
Does this bus go to …?	**Цей автобус їде до …?** [tsɛj aw'tɔbus 'idɛ do …?]
How frequent are the buses?	**Як часто ходять автобуси?** [jak 'tʃasto 'hɔdʲatʲ aw'tɔbusi?]

every 15 minutes	**кожні 15 хвилин** ['kɔʒni pʲjat'nadtsʲatʲ hwi'lin]
every half hour	**щопівгодини** [ɕopiwɦo'dini]
every hour	**щогодини** [ɕoɦo'dini]

several times a day	**кілька разів на день** ['kilʲka ra'ziw na dɛnʲ]
… times a day	**… разів на день** [… ra'ziw na 'dɛnʲ]

schedule	**розклад** ['rɔzklad]
Where can I see the schedule?	**Де можна подивитися розклад?** [dɛ 'mɔʒna podi'witisʲa 'rɔzklad?]

When is the next bus?	**Коли буде наступний автобус?** [ko'li 'budɛ na'stupnij aw'tɔbus?]
When is the first bus?	**Коли відправляється перший автобус?** [ko'li widpraw'lʲaɛtsʲa 'pɛrʃij aw'tɔbus?]
When is the last bus?	**Коли їде останній автобус?** [ko'li 'idɛ os'tanij aw'tɔbus?]

stop	**зупинка** [zu'pinka]
next stop	**наступна зупинка** [na'stupna zu'pinka]
last stop (terminus)	**кінцева зупинка** [kin'tsɛwa zu'pinka]
Stop here, please.	**Зупиніть тут, будь ласка.** [zupiˈnitʲ tut, budʲ 'laska.]
Excuse me, this is my stop.	**Дозвольте, це моя зупинка.** [dozˈwɔlʲtɛ, tsɛ moˈʲa zu'pinka.]

Train

train	**поїзд** ['pɔizd]
suburban train	**приміський поїзд** [prʲimisʲ'kij 'pɔizd]
long-distance train	**поїзд далекого прямування** ['pɔizd da'lɛkoɦo prʲamu'wanʲa]
train station	**вокзал** [wok'zal]
Excuse me, where is the exit to the platform?	**Вибачте, де вихід до поїздів?** ['wibatʃtɛ, dɛ 'wihid do poiz'diw?]

Does this train go to ...?	**Цей поїзд їде до ...?** [tsɛj 'pɔizd 'idɛ do ...?]
next train	**наступний поїзд** [na'stupnij 'pɔizd]
When is the next train?	**Коли буде наступний поїзд?** [ko'lʲi 'budɛ na'stupnij 'pɔizd?]
Where can I see the schedule?	**Де можна подивитися розклад?** [dɛ 'mɔʒna podi'witisʲa 'rɔzklad?]
From which platform?	**З якої платформи?** [z ja'kɔi plat'fɔrmɨ?]
When does the train arrive in ...?	**Коли поїзд прибуває в ...?** [ko'lʲi 'pɔizd pribu'waɛ w ...?]

Please help me.	**Допоможіть мені, будь ласка.** [dopomo'ʒitʲ mɛ'ni, budʲ 'laska.]
I'm looking for my seat.	**Я шукаю своє місце.** [ja ʃu'kaʲu swo'ɛ 'mistsɛ.]
We're looking for our seats.	**Ми шукаємо наші місця.** [mɨ ʃu'kaɛmo 'naʃi mis'tsʲa.]
My seat is taken.	**Моє місце зайняте.** [mo'ɛ 'mistsɛ 'zajnʲatɛ.]
Our seats are taken.	**Наші місця зайняті.** ['naʃi mis'tsʲa 'zajnʲati.]

I'm sorry but this is my seat.	**Вибачте, будь ласка, але це моє місце.** ['wibatʃtɛ, budʲ 'laska, a'lɛ tsɛ mo'ɛ 'mistsɛ.]
Is this seat taken?	**Це місце вільне?** [tsɛ 'mistsɛ 'wilʲnɛ?]
May I sit here?	**Можна мені тут сісти?** ['mɔʒna mɛ'ni tut 'sisti?]

On the train. Dialogue (No ticket)

Ticket, please.
Ваш квиток, будь ласка.
[waʃ kwiˈtɔk, budʲ ˈlaska.]

I don't have a ticket.
У мене немає квитка.
[u ˈmɛnɛ nɛˈmaɛ kwitˈka.]

I lost my ticket.
Я загубив /загубила/ свій квиток.
[ja zaɦuˈbiw /zaɦuˈbila/ swij kwiˈtɔk.]

I forgot my ticket at home.
Я забув /забула/ квиток вдома.
[ja zaˈbuw /zaˈbula/ kwiˈtɔk ˈwdoma.]

You can buy a ticket from me.
Ви можете купити квиток у мене.
[wi ˈmɔʒɛtɛ kuˈpiti kwiˈtɔk u ˈmɛnɛ.]

You will also have to pay a fine.
Вам ще доведеться заплатити штраф.
[wam ɕɛ dowɛˈdɛtʲsʲa zaplaˈtiti ʃtraf.]

Okay.
Добре.
[ˈdɔbrɛ.]

Where are you going?
Куди ви їдете?
[kuˈdi wi ˈidɛtɛ?]

I'm going to …
Я їду до …
[ja ˈidu do …]

How much? I don't understand.
Скільки? Я не розумію.
[ˈskilʲki? ja nɛ rozuˈmiʲu.]

Write it down, please.
Напишіть, будь ласка.
[napiˈʃitʲ, budʲ ˈlaska.]

Okay. Can I pay with a credit card?
Добре. Чи можу я заплатити карткою?
[ˈdɔbrɛ. tʃi ˈmɔʒu ja zaplaˈtiti ˈkartkoʲu?]

Yes, you can.
Так, можете.
[tak, ˈmɔʒɛtɛ.]

Here's your receipt.
Ось ваша квитанція.
[osʲ ˈwaʃa kwiˈtantsiʲa.]

Sorry about the fine.
Шкодую про штраф.
[ʃkoˈduʲu pro ˈʃtraf.]

That's okay. It was my fault.
Це нічого. Це моя вина.
[tsɛ niˈtʃoɦo tsɛ moˈʲa wiˈna.]

Enjoy your trip.
Приємної вам поїздки.
[priˈɛmnoi wam poˈizdki.]

Taxi

taxi	**таксі** [tak'si]
taxi driver	**таксист** [tak'sist]
to catch a taxi	**зловити таксі** [zlo'witi tak'si]
taxi stand	**стоянка таксі** [sto'ʲanka tak'si]
Where can I get a taxi?	**Де я можу взяти таксі?** [dɛ ja 'mɔʒu 'wzʲati tak'si?]

to call a taxi	**викликати таксі** ['wiklikati tak'si]
I need a taxi.	**Мені потрібно таксі.** [mɛ'ni po'tribno tak'si.]
Right now.	**Просто зараз.** ['prɔsto 'zaraz.]
What is your address (location)?	**Ваша адреса?** ['waʃa ad'rɛsa?]
My address is …	**Моя адреса …** [mo'ʲa ad'rɛsa …]
Your destination?	**Куди ви поїдете?** [ku'dɨ wɨ po'idɛtɛ?]

Excuse me, …	**Вибачте, …** ['wibatʃtɛ, …]
Are you available?	**Ви вільні?** [wɨ 'wilʲni?]
How much is it to get to …?	**Скільки коштує доїхати до …?** ['skilʲki 'koʃtuɛ do'ihati do …?]
Do you know where it is?	**Ви знаєте, де це?** [wɨ 'znaɛtɛ, dɛ tsɛ?]

Airport, please.	**В аеропорт, будь ласка.** [w aɛro'port, budʲ 'laska.]
Stop here, please.	**Зупиніться тут, будь ласка.** [zupi'nitʲsʲa tut, budʲ 'laska.]
It's not here.	**Це не тут.** [tsɛ nɛ tut.]
This is the wrong address.	**Це неправильна адреса.** [tsɛ nɛ'prawilʲna ad'rɛsa.]
Turn left.	**Зараз наліво.** ['zaraz na'liwo.]

Turn right.

Зараз направо.
['zaraz na'prawo.]

How much do I owe you?

Скільки я вам винен /винна/?
['skilʲkɨ ja wam 'winɛn /'wina/?]

I'd like a receipt, please.

Дайте мені чек, будь ласка.
['dajtɛ mɛ'ni ʧɛk, budʲ 'laska.]

Keep the change.

Здачі не треба.
['zdaʧi nɛ 'trɛba.]

Would you please wait for me?

Зачекайте мене, будь ласка.
[zaʧɛ'kajtɛ mɛ'nɛ, budʲ 'laska.]

five minutes

5 хвилин
['pʲlatʲ hwɨ'lin]

ten minutes

10 хвилин
['dɛsʲatʲ hwɨ'lin]

fifteen minutes

15 хвилин
[pʲlat'nadʦʲatʲ hwɨ'lin]

twenty minutes

20 хвилин
['dwadʦʲatʲ hwɨ'lin]

half an hour

півгодини
[piwɦo'dinɨ]

Hotel

Hello.	**Добрий день.** ['dɔbrij dɛnʲ.]
My name is …	**Мене звуть …** [mɛ'nɛ zwutʲ …]
I have a reservation.	**Я резервував /резервувала/ номер.** [ja rɛzɛrwu'waw /rɛzɛrwu'wala/ 'nɔmɛr.]
I need …	**Мені потрібен …** [mɛ'ni po'tribɛn …]
a single room	**одномісний номер** [odno'misnij 'nɔmɛr]
a double room	**двомісний номер** [dwo'misnij 'nɔmɛr]
How much is that?	**Скільки він коштує?** ['skilʲki win 'kɔʃtuɛ?]
That's a bit expensive.	**Це трохи дорого.** [ʦɛ 'trɔhi 'dɔroho.]
Do you have anything else?	**У вас є ще що-небудь?** [u was 'ɛ ɕɛ ɕo-'nɛbudʲ?]
I'll take it.	**Я візьму його.** [ja wizʲ'mu ʲo'hɔ.]
I'll pay in cash.	**Я заплачу готівкою.** [ja zapla'ʧu ho'tiwkoʲu.]
I've got a problem.	**У мене є проблема.** [u 'mɛnɛ ɛ prob'lɛma.]
My … is out of order.	**У мене не працює …** [u 'mɛnɛ nɛ pra'ʦʲuɛ …]
TV	**телевізор** [tɛlɛ'wizor]
air conditioner	**кондиціонер** [kondiʦio'nɛr]
tap	**кран** [kran]
shower	**душ** [duʃ]
sink	**раковина** ['rakowina]
safe	**сейф** [sɛjf]
door lock	**замок** [za'mɔk]

electrical outlet	**розетка** [ro'zɛtka]
hairdryer	**фен** [fɛn]

I don't have ...	**У мене немає ...** [u 'mɛnɛ nɛ'maɛ ...]
water	**води** [wo'dɨ]
light	**світла** ['switla]
electricity	**електрики** [ɛ'lɛktrɨkɨ]

Can you give me ...?	**Чи не можете мені дати ...?** [tʃɨ nɛ 'mɔʒɛtɛ mɛ'ni 'datɨ ...?]
a towel	**рушник** [ruʃ'nɨk]
a blanket	**ковдру** ['kɔwdru]
slippers	**тапочки** ['tapotʃkɨ]
a robe	**халат** [ha'lat]
shampoo	**шампунь** [ʃam'punʲ]
soap	**мило** ['mɨlo]

I'd like to change rooms.	**Я б хотів /хотіла/ поміняти номер.** [ja b ho'tiw /ho'tila/ pomi'nʲatɨ 'nɔmɛr.]
I can't find my key.	**Я не можу знайти свій ключ.** [ja nɛ 'mɔʒu znaj'tɨ swij 'klʲutʃ.]
Could you open my room, please?	**Відкрийте мій номер, будь ласка.** [wid'krɨjtɛ mij 'nɔmɛr, budʲ 'laska.]
Who's there?	**Хто там?** [hto tam?]
Come in!	**Заходьте!** [za'hɔdʲtɛ!]
Just a minute!	**Одну хвилину!** [od'nu hwɨ'lɨnu!]
Not right now, please.	**Будь ласка, не зараз.** [budʲ 'laska, nɛ 'zaraz.]

Come to my room, please.	**Зайдіть до мене, будь ласка.** [zaj'ditʲ do 'mɛnɛ, budʲ 'laska.]
I'd like to order food service.	**Я хочу зробити замовлення їжі в номер.** [ja 'hɔtʃu zro'bɨtɨ za'mɔwlɛnja 'iʒi w 'nɔmɛr.]
My room number is ...	**Мій номер кімнати ...** [mij 'nɔmɛr kim'natɨ ...]

I'm leaving …

Я їду …
[ja 'idu …]

We're leaving …

Ми їдемо …
[mɨ 'idɛmo …]

right now

зараз
['zaraz]

this afternoon

сьогодні після обіду
[sʲo'ɦɔdni 'pislʲa o'bidu]

tonight

сьогодні ввечері
[sʲo'ɦɔdni 'wvɛtʃɛri]

tomorrow

завтра
['zawtra]

tomorrow morning

завтра вранці
['zawtra 'wrantsi]

tomorrow evening

завтра ввечері
['zawtra 'wvɛtʃɛri]

the day after tomorrow

післязавтра
[pislʲa'zawtra]

I'd like to pay.

Я б хотів /хотіла/ розрахуватися.
[ja b ho'tiw /ho'tila/ rozrahu'watisʲa.]

Everything was wonderful.

Все було чудово.
[wsɛ bu'lo tʃu'dowo.]

Where can I get a taxi?

Де я можу взяти таксі?
[dɛ ja 'mɔʒu 'wzʲati tak'si?]

Would you call a taxi for me, please?

Викличте мені таксі, будь ласка.
['wɨklɨtʃtɛ mɛ'ni tak'si, budʲ 'laska.]

Restaurant

Can I look at the menu, please?
Чи можу я подивитися ваше меню?
[ʧi 'mɔʒu ja podi'witisʲa 'waʃɛ mɛ'nʲu?]

Table for one.
Столик для одного.
['stɔlik dlʲa od'nɔɦo.]

There are two (three, four) of us.
Нас двоє (троє, четверо).
[nas 'dwɔɛ ('trɔɛ, 'ʧɛtwɛro).]

Smoking
Для курців
[dlʲa kur'ʦiw]

No smoking
Для некурців
[dlʲa nɛkur'ʦiw]

Excuse me! (addressing a waiter)
Будьте ласкаві!
['budʲtɛ las'kawi!]

menu
меню
[mɛ'nʲu]

wine list
карта вин
['karta win]

The menu, please.
Меню, будь ласка.
[mɛ'nʲu, budʲ 'laska.]

Are you ready to order?
Ви готові зробити замовлення?
[wi ɦo'tɔwi zro'biti za'mɔwlɛnʲa?]

What will you have?
Що ви будете замовляти?
[ɕo wi 'budɛtɛ zamow'lʲati?]

I'll have ...
Я буду ...
[ja 'budu ...]

I'm a vegetarian.
Я вегетаріанець /вегетаріанка/.
[ja wɛɦɛtari'anɛʦ /wɛɦɛtari'anka/.]

meat
м'ясо
['mʲaso]

fish
риба
['riba]

vegetables
овочі
['ɔwoʧi]

Do you have vegetarian dishes?
У вас є вегетаріанські страви?
[u was 'ɛ wɛɦɛtari'ansʲki 'strawi?]

I don't eat pork.
Я не їм свинину.
[ja nɛ im swi'ninu.]

He /she/ doesn't eat meat.
Він /вона/ не їсть м'ясо.
[win /wo'na/ nɛ istʲ 'mʲaso.]

I am allergic to ...
У мене алергія на ...
[u 'mɛnɛ alɛr'ɦiʲa na ...]

Would you please bring me …	**Принесіть мені, будь ласка …** [prinɛ'sitʲ mɛ'ni, budʲ 'laska …]
salt | pepper | sugar	**сіль | перець | цукор** [silʲ | 'pɛrɛts | 'tsukor]
coffee | tea | dessert	**каву | чай | десерт** ['kawu | tʃaj | dɛ'sɛrt]
water | sparkling | plain	**воду | з газом | без газу** ['wɔdu | z 'ɦazom | bɛz 'ɦazu]
a spoon | fork | knife	**ложку | вилку | ніж** ['lɔʒku | 'wilku | niʒ]
a plate | napkin	**тарілку | серветку** [ta'rilku | sɛr'wɛtku]

Enjoy your meal!	**Смачного!** [smatʃ'nɔɦo!]
One more, please.	**Принесіть ще, будь ласка.** [prinɛ'sitʲ ɕɛ, budʲ 'laska.]
It was very delicious.	**Було дуже смачно.** [bu'lɔ 'duʒɛ 'smatʃno.]

check | change | tip	**рахунок | здача | чайові** [ra'hunok | 'zdatʃa | tʃaʲo'wi]
Check, please. (Could I have the check, please?)	**Рахунок, будь ласка.** [ra'hunok, budʲ 'laska.]
Can I pay by credit card?	**Чи можу я заплатити карткою?** [tʃɨ 'mɔʒu ja zapla'tɨtɨ 'kartkoʲu?]
I'm sorry, there's a mistake here.	**Вибачте, тут помилка.** ['wɨbatʃtɛ, tut po'mɨlka.]

Shopping

Can I help you?
Чи можу я вам допомогти?
[tʃi 'mɔʒu ja wam dopomoɦ'ti?]

Do you have ...?
У вас є ...?
[u was 'ɛ ...?]

I'm looking for ...
Я шукаю ...
[ja ʃu'kaʲu ...]

I need ...
Мені потрібен ...
[mɛ'ni po'tribɛn ...]

I'm just looking.
Я просто дивлюся.
[ja 'prɔsto 'diwlʲusʲa.]

We're just looking.
Ми просто дивимося.
[mi 'prɔsto 'diwimosʲa.]

I'll come back later.
Я зайду пізніше.
[ja zaj'du piz'niʃɛ.]

We'll come back later.
Ми зайдемо пізніше.
[mi 'zajdɛmo piz'niʃɛ.]

discounts | sale
знижки | розпродаж
['zniʒki | roz'prodaʒ]

Would you please show me ...
Покажіть мені, будь ласка ...
[poka'ʒitʲ mɛ'ni, budʲ 'laska ...]

Would you please give me ...
Дайте мені, будь ласка ...
['dajtɛ mɛ'ni, budʲ 'laska ...]

Can I try it on?
Чи можна мені це приміряти?
[tʃi 'mɔʒna mɛ'ni tsɛ pri'mirʲati?]

Excuse me, where's the fitting room?
Вибачте, де примірювальна?
['wibatʃtɛ, dɛ pri'mirʲuwalʲna?]

Which color would you like?
Який колір ви хочете?
[ja'kij 'kɔlir wi 'hotʃɛtɛ?]

size | length
розмір | зріст
['rɔzmir | zrist]

How does it fit?
Підійшло?
[pidij'ʃlɔ?]

How much is it?
Скільки це коштує?
['skilʲki tsɛ 'koʃtuɛ?]

That's too expensive.
Це занадто дорого.
[tsɛ za'nadto 'dɔroɦo.]

I'll take it.
Я візьму це.
[ja wizʲ'mu tsɛ.]

Excuse me, where do I pay?
Вибачте, де каса?
['wibatʃtɛ, dɛ 'kasa?]

Will you pay in cash or credit card?

Як ви будете платити? Готівкою чи кредиткою?
[jak wɨ 'budɛtɛ pla'tɨtɨ? ɦo'tiwkoʲu ʧɨ krɛ'dɨtkoʲu?]

In cash | with credit card

готівкою | карткою
[ɦo'tiwkoʲu | 'kartkoʲu]

Do you want the receipt?

Вам потрібен чек?
[wam po'tribɛn ʧɛk?]

Yes, please.

Так, будьте ласкаві.
[tak, 'budʲtɛ las'kawi.]

No, it's OK.

Ні, не потрібно. Дякую.
[ni, nɛ po'tribno. 'dʲakuʲu.]

Thank you. Have a nice day!

Дякую. На все добре!
['dʲakuʲu. na wsɛ 'dɔbrɛ.]

In town

Excuse me, please.	**Вибачте, будь ласка …** ['wibatʃtɛ, budʲ 'laska …]
I'm looking for …	**Я шукаю …** [ja ʃu'kaʲu …]

the subway	**метро** [mɛt'rɔ]
my hotel	**свій готель** [swij ɦo'tɛlʲ]
the movie theater	**кінотеатр** [kinotɛ'atr]
a taxi stand	**стоянку таксі** [sto'ʲanku tak'si]

an ATM	**банкомат** [banko'mat]
a foreign exchange office	**обмін валют** ['ɔbmin wa'lʲut]
an internet café	**інтернет-кафе** [intɛr'nɛt-ka'fɛ]
… street	**вулицю …** ['wulitsʲu …]
this place	**ось це місце** [osʲ tsɛ 'mistsɛ]

Do you know where … is?	**Чи не знаєте Ви, де знаходиться …?** [tʃi nɛ 'znaɛtɛ wi, dɛ zna'ɦoditʲsʲa …?]
Which street is this?	**Як називається ця вулиця?** [jak nazi'waɛtʲsʲa tsʲa 'wulitsʲa?]
Show me where we are right now.	**Покажіть, де ми зараз.** [poka'ʒitʲ, dɛ mi 'zaraz.]

Can I get there on foot?	**Я дійду туди пішки?** [ja dij'du tu'di 'piʃki?]
Do you have a map of the city?	**У вас є карта міста?** [u was 'ɛ 'karta 'mista?]

How much is a ticket to get in?	**Скільки коштує вхідний квиток?** ['skilʲki 'koʃtuɛ whid'nij kwi'tɔk?]
Can I take pictures here?	**Чи можна тут фотографувати?** [tʃi 'moʒna tut fotoɦrafu'wati?]
Are you open?	**Ви відкриті?** [wi widk'riti?]

When do you open? | **О котрій ви відкриваєтесь?**
[o kot'rij wɨ widkrɨ'waɛtɛsʲ?]

When do you close? | **До котрої години ви працюєте?**
[do ko'trɔi ɦo'dɨnɨ wɨ pra'tsʲuɛtɛ?]

Money

money	гроші
	['ɦrɔʃi]
cash	готівкові гроші
	[ɦotiw'kɔwi 'ɦrɔʃi]
paper money	паперові гроші
	[papɛ'rɔwi 'ɦrɔʃi]
loose change	дрібні гроші
	[drib'ni 'ɦrɔʃi]
check | change | tip	рахунок | здача | чайові
	[ra'ɦunok | 'zdatʃa | tʃaʲo'wi]

credit card	кредитна картка
	[krɛ'dɨtna 'kartka]
wallet	гаманець
	[ɦama'nɛts]
to buy	купувати
	[kupu'watɨ]
to pay	платити
	[pla'tɨtɨ]
fine	штраф
	['ʃtraf]
free	безкоштовно
	[bɛzkoʃ'tɔwno]

Where can I buy ...?	Де я можу купити ...?
	[dɛ ja 'mɔʒu ku'pɨtɨ ...?]
Is the bank open now?	Чи відкритий зараз банк?
	[tʃɨ wid'krɨtɨj 'zaraz bank?]
When does it open?	О котрій він відкривається?
	[o kot'rij wɨn widkrɨ'waɛtʲsʲa?]
When does it close?	До котрої години він працює?
	[do ko'trɔi ɦo'dɨnɨ wɨn pra'tsʲuɛ?]

How much?	Скільки?
	['skilʲkɨ?]
How much is this?	Скільки це коштує?
	['skilʲkɨ tsɛ 'kɔʃtuɛ?]
That's too expensive.	Це занадто дорого.
	[tsɛ za'nadto 'dɔroɦo.]

Excuse me, where do I pay?	Вибачте, де каса?
	['wɨbatʃtɛ, dɛ 'kasa?]
Check, please.	Рахунок, будь ласка.
	[ra'ɦunok, budʲ 'laska.]

Can I pay by credit card?

Чи можу я заплатити карткою?
[tʃi 'mɔʒu ja zapla'titi 'kartkoʲu?]

Is there an ATM here?

Тут є банкомат?
[tut ɛ banko'mat?]

I'm looking for an ATM.

Мені потрібен банкомат.
[mɛ'ni po'tribɛn banko'mat.]

I'm looking for a foreign exchange office.

Я шукаю обмін валют.
[ja ʃu'kaʲu 'ɔbmin wa'lʲut.]

I'd like to change …

Я б хотів /хотіла/ поміняти …
[ja b ho'tiw /ho'tila/ pomi'nʲati …]

What is the exchange rate?

Який курс обміну?
[ja'kij kurs 'ɔbminu?]

Do you need my passport?

Вам потрібен мій паспорт?
[wam po'tribɛn mij 'pasport?]

Time

What time is it?	**Котра година?** [ko'tra ɦo'dina?]
When?	**Коли?** [ko'lɨ?]
At what time?	**О котрій?** [o kot'rij?]
now | later | after ...	**зараз | пізніше | після ...** ['zaraz | piz'niʃɛ | 'pislʲa ...]
one o'clock	**перша година дня** ['pɛrʃa ɦo'dina dnʲa]
one fifteen	**п'ятнадцять на другу** [pʲat'nadtsʲatʲ na 'druɦu]
one thirty	**половина другої** [polo'wina 'druɦoi]
one forty-five	**за п'ятнадцять друга** [za pʲat'nattsʲatʲ 'druɦa]

one | two | three	**один | два | три** [o'din | dwa | trɨ]
four | five | six	**чотири | п'ять | шість** [tʃo'tiri | 'pʲatʲ | ʃistʲ]
seven | eight | nine	**сім | вісім | дев'ять** [sim | 'wisim | 'dɛwʲatʲ]
ten | eleven | twelve	**десять | одинадцять | дванадцять** ['dɛsʲatʲ | odɨ'nadtsʲatʲ | dwa'nadtsʲatʲ]

in ...	**через ...** ['tʃɛrɛz ...]
five minutes	**5 хвилин** ['pʲatʲ hwɨ'lin]
ten minutes	**10 хвилин** ['dɛsʲatʲ hwɨ'lin]
fifteen minutes	**15 хвилин** [pʲat'nadtsʲatʲ hwɨ'lin]
twenty minutes	**20 хвилин** ['dwadtsʲatʲ hwɨ'lin]
half an hour	**півгодини** [piwɦo'dini]
an hour	**одна година** [od'na ɦo'dina]
in the morning	**вранці** ['wrantsi]
early in the morning	**рано вранці** ['rano 'wrantsi]

this morning	сьогодні вранці
	[sʲo'hɔdni 'wrantsi]
tomorrow morning	завтра вранці
	['zawtra 'wrantsi]

in the middle of the day	в обід
	[w o'bid]
in the afternoon	після обіду
	['pislʲa o'bidu]
in the evening	ввечері
	['wvɛtʃɛri]
tonight	сьогодні ввечері
	[sʲo'hɔdni 'wvɛtʃɛri]

at night	вночі
	[wno'tʃi]
yesterday	вчора
	['wtʃɔra]
today	сьогодні
	[sʲo'hɔdni]
tomorrow	завтра
	['zawtra]
the day after tomorrow	післязавтра
	[pislʲa'zawtra]

What day is it today?	Який сьогодні день?
	[ja'kij sʲo'hɔdni dɛnʲ?]
It's …	Сьогодні …
	[sʲo'hɔdni …]
Monday	понеділок
	[ponɛ'dilok]
Tuesday	вівторок
	[wiw'tɔrok]
Wednesday	середа
	[sɛrɛ'da]

Thursday	четвер
	[tʃɛt'wɛr]
Friday	п'ятниця
	['pʲatnitsʲa]
Saturday	субота
	[su'bɔta]
Sunday	неділя
	[nɛ'dilʲa]

Greetings. Introductions

Hello.	**Добрий день.** ['dɔbrij dɛnʲ.]
Pleased to meet you.	**Радий /рада/ з вами познайомитися.** ['radij /'rada/ z 'wamɨ pozna'jɔmɨtisʲa.]
Me too.	**Я теж.** [ja tɛʒ.]
I'd like you to meet …	**Знайомтеся. Це …** [zna'jɔmtɛsʲa. tsɛ …]
Nice to meet you.	**Дуже приємно.** ['duʒɛ prɨ'ɛmno.]

How are you?	**Як ви? Як у вас справи?** [jak wɨ? jak u was 'sprawɨ?]
My name is …	**Мене звуть …** [mɛ'nɛ zwutʲ …]
His name is …	**Його звуть …** [ʲo'hɔ zwutʲ …]
Her name is …	**Її звуть …** [iɨ 'zwutʲ …]

What's your name?	**Як вас звуть?** [jak was 'zwutʲ?]
What's his name?	**Як його звуть?** [jak ʲo'hɔ zwutʲ?]
What's her name?	**Як її звуть?** [jak iɨ 'zwutʲ?]

What's your last name?	**Яке ваше прізвище?** [ja'kɛ 'waʃɛ 'prizwɨɕɛ?]
You can call me …	**Називайте мене …** [nazɨ'wajtɛ mɛ'nɛ …]
Where are you from?	**Звідки ви?** ['zwidkɨ wɨ?]
I'm from …	**Я з …** [ja z …]
What do you do for a living?	**Ким ви працюєте?** [kɨm wɨ pra'tsʲuɛtɛ?]

Who is this?	**Хто це?** [hto tsɛ?]
Who is he?	**Хто він?** [hto win?]
Who is she?	**Хто вона?** [hto wo'na?]

Who are they?	**Хто вони?** [hto wo'nɨ?]
This is …	**Це …** [ʦɛ …]
my friend (masc.)	**мій друг** [mij druɦ]
my friend (fem.)	**моя подруга** [mo'ʲa 'pɔdruɦa]
my husband	**мій чоловік** [mij ʧolo'wik]
my wife	**моя дружина** [mo'ʲa dru'ʒɨna]
my father	**мій батько** [mij 'batʲko]
my mother	**моя мама** [mo'ʲa 'mama]
my brother	**мій брат** [mij brat]
my sister	**моя сестра** [mo'ʲa sɛst'ra]
my son	**мій син** [mij sɨn]
my daughter	**моя дочка** [mo'ʲa doʧ'ka]
This is our son.	**Це наш син.** [ʦɛ naʃ sɨn.]
This is our daughter.	**Це наша дочка.** [ʦɛ 'naʃa doʧ'ka.]
These are my children.	**Це мої діти.** [ʦɛ mo'i 'dit̪ɨ.]
These are our children.	**Це наші діти.** [ʦɛ 'naʃi 'dit̪ɨ.]

Farewells

Good bye!
До побачення!
[do po'batʃɛnʲa!]

Bye! (inform.)
Бувай!
[bu'waj!]

See you tomorrow.
До завтра.
[do 'zawtra.]

See you soon.
До зустрічі.
[do 'zustritʃi.]

See you at seven.
Зустрінемось о сьомій.
[zust'rinɛmosʲ o 'sʲɔmij.]

Have fun!
Розважайтеся!
[rozwa'ʒajtɛsʲa!]

Talk to you later.
Поговоримо пізніше.
[poɦo'wɔrimo piz'niʃɛ.]

Have a nice weekend.
Вдалих вихідних.
['wdaliɦ wiɦid'niɦ.]

Good night.
На добраніч.
[na do'branitʃ.]

It's time for me to go.
Мені вже час.
[mɛ'ni wʒɛ tʃas.]

I have to go.
Мушу йти.
['muʃu jti.]

I will be right back.
Я зараз повернусь.
[ja 'zaraz powɛr'nusʲ.]

It's late.
Вже пізно.
[wʒɛ 'pizno.]

I have to get up early.
Мені рано вставати.
[mɛ'ni 'rano wsta'wati.]

I'm leaving tomorrow.
Я завтра від'їжджаю.
[ja 'zawtra widʲiʒ'dʒaʲu.]

We're leaving tomorrow.
Ми завтра від'їжджаємо.
[mɨ 'zawtra widʲiʒ'dʒaɛmo.]

Have a nice trip!
Щасливої поїздки!
[ɕas'liwoi po'izdki!]

It was nice meeting you.
Було приємно з вами познайомитися.
[bu'lɔ prɨ'ɛmno z 'wamɨ pozna'jɔmitisʲa.]

It was nice talking to you.

Було приємно з вами поспілкуватися.
[bu'lɔ pri'ɛmno z 'wamɨ pospilku'watisʲa.]

Thanks for everything.

Дякую за все.
['dʲakuʲu za wsɛ.]

I had a very good time.

Я чудово провів /провела/ час.
[ja tʃu'dɔwo pro'wiw /prowɛ'la/ tʃas.]

We had a very good time.

Ми чудово провели час.
[mɨ tʃu'dɔwo prowɛ'lɨ tʃas.]

It was really great.

Все було чудово.
[wsɛ bu'lɔ tʃu'dɔwo.]

I'm going to miss you.

Я буду сумувати.
[ja 'budu sumu'watɨ.]

We're going to miss you.

Ми будемо сумувати.
[mɨ 'budɛmo sumu'watɨ.]

Good luck!

Успіхів! Щасливо!
['uspihiw! ɕas'lɨwo!]

Say hi to …

Передавайте вітання …
[pɛrɛda'wajtɛ wi'tanʲa …]

Foreign language

I don't understand.	**Я не розумію.** [ja nɛ rozu'mіʲu.]
Write it down, please.	**Напишіть це, будь ласка.** [napiʲʃitʲ tsɛ, budʲ 'laska.]
Do you speak ...?	**Ви знаєте ...?** [wɨ 'znaɛtɛ ...?]

I speak a little bit of ...	**Я трохи знаю ...** [ja 'trɔhɨ znaʲu ...]
English	**англійська** [anʰ'lijsʲka]
Turkish	**турецька** [tu'rɛtska]
Arabic	**арабська** [a'rabsʲka]
French	**французька** [fran'tsuzʲka]

German	**німецька** [ni'mɛtska]
Italian	**італійська** [ita'lijsʲka]
Spanish	**іспанська** [is'pansʲka]
Portuguese	**португальська** [portu'ɦalʲsʲka]
Chinese	**китайська** [kɨ'tajsʲka]
Japanese	**японська** [ja'pɔnsʲka]

Can you repeat that, please.	**Повторіть, будь ласка.** [powto'ritʲ, budʲ 'laska.]
I understand.	**Я розумію.** [ja rozu'mіʲu.]
I don't understand.	**Я не розумію.** [ja nɛ rozu'mіʲu.]
Please speak more slowly.	**Говоріть повільніше, будь ласка.** [ɦowo'ritʲ po'wilʲniʃɛ, 'budʲ 'laska.]

Is that correct? (Am I saying it right?)	**Це правильно?** [tsɛ 'prawɨlʲno?]
What is this? (What does this mean?)	**Що це?** [ɕo 'tsɛ?]

Apologies

Excuse me, please.

Вибачте, будь ласка.
['wibatʃtɛ, budⁱ 'laska.]

I'm sorry.

Мені шкода.
[mɛ'ni 'ʃkɔda.]

I'm really sorry.

Мені дуже шкода.
[mɛ'ni 'duʒɛ 'ʃkɔda.]

Sorry, it's my fault.

Винен /Винна/, це моя вина.
['winɛn /'wina/ , ʦɛ mo'ⁱa wi'na.]

My mistake.

Моя помилка.
[mo'ⁱa po'milka.]

May I ...?

Чи можу я ...?
[ʧi 'mɔʒu ja ...?]

Do you mind if I ...?

Ви не заперечуватимете, якщо я ...?
[wi nɛ zapɛ'rɛʧuwatimɛtɛ, jak'ɕɔ ja ...?]

It's OK.

Нічого страшного.
[ni'ʧɔho straʃ'nɔho.]

It's all right.

Все гаразд.
[wsɛ ɦa'razd.]

Don't worry about it.

Не турбуйтесь.
[nɛ tur'bujtɛsⁱ.]

Agreement

Yes.	**Так.** [tak.]
Yes, sure.	**Так, звичайно.** [tak, zwɨ'ʧajno.]
OK (Good!)	**Добре!** ['dɔbrɛ!]
Very well.	**Дуже добре.** ['duʒɛ 'dɔbrɛ.]
Certainly!	**Звичайно!** [zwɨ'ʧajno!]
I agree.	**Я згідний /згідна/.** [ja 'zɦidnɨj /'zɦidna/.]

That's correct.	**Вірно.** ['wirno.]
That's right.	**Правильно.** ['prawɨlʲno.]
You're right.	**Ви праві.** [wɨ pra'wi.]
I don't mind.	**Я не заперечую.** [ja nɛ zapɛ'rɛʧuʲu.]
Absolutely right.	**Абсолютно вірно.** [abso'lʲutno 'wirno.]

It's possible.	**Це можливо.** [ʦɛ moʒ'lɨwo.]
That's a good idea.	**Це гарна думка.** [ʦɛ 'ɦarna 'dumka.]
I can't say no.	**Не можу відмовити.** [nɛ 'mɔʒu wid'mɔwɨtɨ.]
I'd be happy to.	**Буду радий /рада/.** ['budu 'radɨj /'rada/.]
With pleasure.	**Із задоволенням.** [iz zado'wɔlɛnjam.]

Refusal. Expressing doubt

No.	**Ні.** [ni.]
Certainly not.	**Звичайно, ні.** [zwɨ'tʃajno, ni.]
I don't agree.	**Я не згідний /згідна/.** [ja nɛ 'zɦidnɨj /'zɦidna/.]

I don't think so.	**Я так не думаю.** [ja tak nɛ 'dumaʲu.]
It's not true.	**Це неправда.** [ʦɛ nɛ'prawda.]

You are wrong.	**Ви неправі.** [wɨ nɛpra'wi.]
I think you are wrong.	**Я думаю, що ви неправі.** [ja 'dumaʲu, ɕo wɨ nɛpra'wi.]
I'm not sure.	**Не впевнений /впевнена/.** [nɛ 'wpɛwnɛnɨj /'wpɛwnɛna/.]

It's impossible.	**Це неможливо.** [ʦɛ nɛmoʒ'lɨwo.]
Nothing of the kind (sort)!	**Нічого подібного!** [ni'tʃoɦo po'dibnoɦo!]

The exact opposite.	**Навпаки!** [nawpa'kɨ!]
I'm against it.	**Я проти.** [ja 'protɨ.]

I don't care.	**Мені все одно.** [mɛ'ni wsɛ od'nɔ.]
I have no idea.	**Гадки не маю.** ['ɦadkɨ nɛ 'maʲu.]
I doubt it.	**Сумніваюся, що це так.** [sumni'waʲusʲa, ɕo ʦɛ tak.]

Sorry, I can't.	**Вибачте, я не можу.** ['wɨbatʃtɛ, ja nɛ 'mɔʒu.]
Sorry, I don't want to.	**Вибачте, я не хочу.** ['wɨbatʃtɛ, ja nɛ 'hɔtʃu.]
Thank you, but I don't need this.	**Дякую, мені це не потрібно.** ['dʲakuʲu, mɛ'ni ʦɛ nɛ pot'ribno.]
It's getting late.	**Вже пізно.** [wʒɛ 'pizno.]

I have to get up early.

Мені рано вставати.
[mɛˈni ˈrano wstaˈwati.]

I don't feel well.

Я погано себе почуваю.
[ja poˈɦano sɛˈbɛ potʃuˈwaʲu.]

Expressing gratitude

Thank you.	**Дякую.** ['dʲakuʲu.]
Thank you very much.	**Дуже дякую.** ['duʒɛ 'dʲakuʲu.]
I really appreciate it.	**Дуже вдячний /вдячна/.** ['duʒɛ 'wdʲatʃnij /'wdʲatʃna/.]
I'm really grateful to you.	**Я вам вдячний /вдячна/.** [ja wam 'wdʲatʃnij /'wdʲatʃna/.]
We are really grateful to you.	**Ми Вам вдячні.** [mɨ wam 'wdʲatʃni.]

Thank you for your time.	**Дякую, що витратили час.** ['dʲakuʲu, ɕo 'wɨtratɨlɨ tʃas.]
Thanks for everything.	**Дякую за все.** ['dʲakuʲu za wsɛ.]
Thank you for ...	**Дякую за ...** ['dʲakuʲu za ...]
your help	**вашу допомогу** ['waʃu dopo'mɔɦu]
a nice time	**гарний час** ['ɦarnij tʃas]

a wonderful meal	**чудову їжу** [tʃu'dɔwu 'iʒu]
a pleasant evening	**приємний вечір** [prɨ'ɛmnɨj 'wɛtʃir]
a wonderful day	**чудовий день** [tʃu'dɔwɨj dɛnʲ]
an amazing journey	**цікаву екскурсію** [tsi'kawu ɛks'kursiʲu]

Don't mention it.	**Нема за що.** [nɛ'ma za ɕo.]
You are welcome.	**Не варто дякувати.** [nɛ 'warto 'dʲakuwatɨ.]
Any time.	**Завжди будь ласка.** [za'wʒdɨ budʲ 'laska.]
My pleasure.	**Був радий /Була рада/ допомогти.** [buw 'radɨj /bu'la 'rada/ dopomoɦ'tɨ.]
Forget it.	**Забудьте. Все гаразд.** [za'budʲtɛ wsɛ ɦa'razd.]
Don't worry about it.	**Не турбуйтесь.** [nɛ tur'bujtɛsʲ.]

Congratulations. Best wishes

Congratulations!	**Вітаю!** [wi'taʲu!]
Happy birthday!	**З Днем народження!** [z dnɛm na'rɔdʒɛnʲa!]
Merry Christmas!	**Веселого Різдва!** [wɛ'sɛloɦo rizd'wa!]
Happy New Year!	**З Новим роком!** [z no'wim 'rɔkom!]
Happy Easter!	**Зі Світлим Великоднем!** [zi 'switlim wɛ'likodnɛm!]
Happy Hanukkah!	**Щасливої Хануки!** [ɕas'liwoi ha'nuki!]
I'd like to propose a toast.	**У мене є тост.** [u 'mɛnɛ ɛ tost.]
Cheers!	**За ваше здоров'я!** [za 'waʃɛ zdo'rɔwʲa]
Let's drink to …!	**Вип'ємо за …!** ['wipʲɛmo za …!]
To our success!	**За наш успіх!** [za naʃ 'uspih!]
To your success!	**За ваш успіх!** [za waʃ 'uspih!]
Good luck!	**Успіхів!** ['uspihiw!]
Have a nice day!	**Гарного вам дня!** ['ɦarnoɦo wam dnʲa!]
Have a good holiday!	**Гарного вам відпочинку!** ['ɦarnoɦo wam widpo'tʃinku!]
Have a safe journey!	**Вдалої поїздки!** ['wdaloi po'izdki!]
I hope you get better soon!	**Бажаю вам швидкого одужання!** [ba'ʒaʲu wam ʃwid'kɔɦo o'duʒanʲa!]

Socializing

Why are you sad?	**Чому ви засмучені?** [ʧɔ'mu wɨ zas'muʧɛni?]
Smile! Cheer up!	**Посміхніться!** [posmih'nitʲsʲaǃ]
Are you free tonight?	**Ви не зайняті сьогодні ввечері?** [wɨ nɛ 'zajnʲati sʲo'ɦodni 'wwɛʧɛri?]

May I offer you a drink?	**Чи можу я запропонувати вам випити?** [ʧɨ 'mɔʒu ja zaproponu'watɨ wam 'wipɨtɨ?]
Would you like to dance?	**Чи не хочете потанцювати?** [ʧɨ nɛ 'hɔʧɛtɛ potantsʲu'watɨ?]
Let's go to the movies.	**Може сходимо в кіно?** ['mɔʒɛ 'shɔdimo w ki'nɔ?]

May I invite you to …?	**Чи можна запросити вас в …?** [ʧɨ 'mɔʒna zapro'sɨtɨ was w …?]
a restaurant	**ресторан** [rɛsto'ran]
the movies	**кіно** [ki'nɔ]
the theater	**театр** [tɛ'atr]
go for a walk	**на прогулянку** [na pro'ɦulʲanku]

At what time?	**О котрій?** [o kot'rij?]
tonight	**сьогодні ввечері** [sʲo'ɦodni 'wwɛʧɛri]
at six	**о 6 годині** [o 'ʃɔstij ɦo'dini]
at seven	**о 7 годині** [o 'sʲɔmij ɦo'dini]
at eight	**о 8 годині** [o 'wɔsʲmij ɦo'dini]
at nine	**о 9 годині** [o dɛ'wʲˈatij ɦo'dini]

Do you like it here?	**Вам тут подобається?** [wam tut po'dɔbaɛtʲsʲa?]
Are you here with someone?	**Ви тут з кимось?** [wɨ tut z 'kɨmosʲ?]

I'm with my friend.
Я з другом /подругою/.
[ja z 'druɦom /'pɔdruɦoʲu/.]

I'm with my friends.
Я з друзями.
[ja z 'druzʲamɨ.]

No, I'm alone.
Я один /одна/.
[ja o'dɨn /od'na/.]

Do you have a boyfriend?
У тебе є приятель?
[u 'tɛbɛ ɛ 'prɨjatɛlʲ?]

I have a boyfriend.
У мене є друг.
[u 'mɛnɛ ɛ druɦ.]

Do you have a girlfriend?
У тебе є подружка?
[u 'tɛbɛ ɛ 'pɔdruʒka?]

I have a girlfriend.
У мене є дівчина.
[u 'mɛnɛ ɛ 'diwtʃɨna.]

Can I see you again?
Ми ще зустрінемося?
[mɨ ɕɛ zu'strinɛmosʲa?]

Can I call you?
Чи можна тобі подзвонити?
[tʃɨ 'mɔʒna to'bi zatɛlɛfonu'watɨ?]

Call me. (Give me a call.)
Подзвони мені.
[podzwo'nɨ mɛ'ni.]

What's your number?
Який у тебе номер?
[ja'kɨj u 'tɛbɛ 'nɔmɛr?]

I miss you.
Я сумую за тобою.
[ja su'muʲu za to'bɔʲu.]

You have a beautiful name.
У вас дуже гарне ім'я.
[u was 'duʒɛ 'ɦarnɛ i'mʲˀa.]

I love you.
Я тебе кохаю.
[ja tɛbɛ ko'haʲu.]

Will you marry me?
Виходь за мене.
[wɨ'hɔdʲ za 'mɛnɛ.]

You're kidding!
Ви жартуєте!
[wɨ ʒar'tuɛtɛ!]

I'm just kidding.
Я просто жартую.
[ja 'prɔsto ʒar'tuʲu.]

Are you serious?
Ви серйозно?
[wɨ sɛr'jɔzno?]

I'm serious.
Я серйозно.
[ja sɛr'jɔzno.]

Really?!
Справді?!
['sprawdi?!]

It's unbelievable!
Це неймовірно!
[tsɛ nɛjmo'wirno]

I don't believe you.
Я вам не вірю.
[ja wam nɛ 'wirʲu.]

I can't.
Я не можу.
[ja nɛ 'mɔʒu.]

I don't know.
Я не знаю.
[ja nɛ 'znaʲu.]

I don't understand you.

Я вас не розумію.
[ja was nɛ rozu'miʲu.]

Please go away.

Ідіть, будь ласка.
[i'ditʲ, budʲ 'laska.]

Leave me alone!

Залиште мене в спокої!
[za'liʃtɛ mɛ'nɛ w 'spɔkoi!]

I can't stand him.

Я його терпіти не можу.
[ja ʲo'hɔ tɛr'piti nɛ 'mɔʒu.]

You are disgusting!

Ви огидні!
[wɨ o'ɦidni!]

I'll call the police!

Я викличу поліцію!
[ja 'wɨklitʃu po'litsiʲu!]

Sharing impressions. Emotions

I like it.	**Мені це подобається.** [mɛ'ni ʦɛ po'dɔbaɛtʲsʲa.]
Very nice.	**Дуже мило.** ['duʒɛ 'miɫo.]
That's great!	**Це чудово!** [ʦɛ ʧu'dɔwo!]
It's not bad.	**Це непогано.** [ʦɛ nɛpo'ɦano.]

I don't like it.	**Мені це не подобається.** [mɛ'ni ʦɛ nɛ po'dɔbaɛtʲsʲa.]
It's not good.	**Це недобре.** [ʦɛ nɛ'dɔbrɛ.]
It's bad.	**Це погано.** [ʦɛ po'ɦano.]
It's very bad.	**Це дуже погано.** [ʦɛ 'duʒɛ po'ɦano.]
It's disgusting.	**Це огидно.** [ʦɛ o'ɦidno.]

I'm happy.	**Я щасливий /щаслива/.** [ja ɕas'liwij /ɕas'liwa/.]
I'm content.	**Я задоволений /задоволена/.** [ja zado'wolɛnij /zado'wolɛna/.]
I'm in love.	**Я закоханий /закохана/.** [ja za'kɔhanij /za'kɔhana/.]
I'm calm.	**Я спокійний /спокійна/.** [ja spo'kijnij /spo'kijna/.]
I'm bored.	**Мені нудно.** [mɛ'ni 'nudno.]

I'm tired.	**Я втомився /втомилася/.** [ja wto'miwsʲa /wto'miɫasʲa/.]
I'm sad.	**Мені сумно.** [mɛ'ni 'sumno.]
I'm frightened.	**Я наляканий /налякана/.** [ja na'lʲakanij /na'lʲakana/.]

I'm angry.	**Я злюся.** [ja 'zlʲusʲa.]
I'm worried.	**Я хвилююся.** [ja hwi'lʲulʲusʲa.]
I'm nervous.	**Я нервую.** [ja nɛr'wulʲu.]

I'm jealous. (envious)

Я заздрю.
[ja 'zazdrʲu.]

I'm surprised.

Я здивований /здивована/.
[ja zdʲi'wɔwanij /zdʲi'wɔwana/.]

I'm perplexed.

Я спантеличений /спантеличена/.
[ja spantɛ'litʃɛnij /spantɛ'litʃɛna/.]

Problems. Accidents

I've got a problem.

В мене проблема.
[w 'mɛnɛ prob'lɛma.]

We've got a problem.

У нас проблема.
[u nas prob'lɛma.]

I'm lost.

Я заблукав /заблукала/.
[ja zablu'kaw /zablu'kala/.]

I missed the last bus (train).

Я запізнився на останній автобус (поїзд).
[ja zapiz'niwsʲa na os'tanij aw'tɔbus ('pɔizd).]

I don't have any money left.

У мене зовсім не залишилося грошей.
[u 'mɛnɛ 'zɔwsim nɛ za'liʃilosʲa 'hrɔʃɛj.]

I've lost my ...

Я загубив /загубила/ ...
[ja zaɦu'biw /zaɦu'biła/ ...]

Someone stole my ...

В мене вкрали ...
[w 'mɛnɛ 'wkrali ...]

passport

паспорт
['pasport]

wallet

гаманець
[ɦama'nɛts]

papers

документи
[doku'mɛnti]

ticket

квиток
[kwi'tɔk]

money

гроші
['ɦrɔʃi]

handbag

сумку
['sumku]

camera

фотоапарат
[fotoapa'rat]

laptop

ноутбук
[nout'buk]

tablet computer

планшет
[plan'ʃet]

mobile phone

телефон
[tɛlɛ'fɔn]

Help me!

Допоможіть!
[dopomo'ʒitʲ]

What's happened?

Що трапилося?
[ɕo 'trapiłosʲa?]

fire	**пожежа** [po'ʒɛʒa]
shooting	**стрілянина** [strilʲa'nina]
murder	**вбивство** ['wbiwstwo]
explosion	**вибух** ['wibuh]
fight	**бійка** ['bijka]

Call the police!	**Викличте поліцію!** ['wiklitʃtɛ po'litsiʲu!]
Please hurry up!	**Будь ласка, швидше!** [budʲ 'laska, 'ʃwidʃɛ!]
I'm looking for the police station.	**Я шукаю поліцейську дільницю.** [ja ʃu'kaʲu poli'tsɛjsʲku dilʲ'nitsʲu.]
I need to make a call.	**Мені треба зателефонувати.** [mɛ'ni 'trɛba zatɛlɛfonu'wati.]
May I use your phone?	**Чи можна мені зателефонувати?** [tʃi 'moʒna mɛ'ni zatɛlɛfonu'wati?]

I've been …	**Мене …** [mɛ'nɛ …]
mugged	**пограбували** [pohrabu'wali]
robbed	**обікрали** [obi'krali]
raped	**зґвалтували** [zgwaltu'wali]
attacked (beaten up)	**побили** [po'bili]

Are you all right?	**З вами все гаразд?** [z 'wami wsɛ ha'razd?]
Did you see who it was?	**Ви бачили, хто це був?** [wi 'batʃili, hto tsɛ buw?]
Would you be able to recognize the person?	**Ви зможете його впізнати?** [wi 'zmoʒɛtɛ ʲo'ho wpiz'nati?]
Are you sure?	**Ви точно впевнені?** [wi 'totʃno 'wpɛwnɛni?]

Please calm down.	**Будь ласка, заспокойтеся.** [budʲ 'laska, zaspo'kojtɛsʲa.]
Take it easy!	**Спокійніше!** [spokij'niʃɛ!]
Don't worry!	**Не турбуйтесь.** [nɛ tur'bujtɛsʲ.]
Everything will be fine.	**Все буде добре.** [wsɛ 'budɛ 'dobrɛ.]
Everything's all right.	**Все гаразд.** [wsɛ ha'razd.]

Come here, please.

Підійдіть, будь ласка.
[pidij'ditʲ, budʲ 'laska.]

I have some questions for you.

У мене до вас кілька запитань.
[u 'mɛnɛ do was 'kilʲka zapi'tanʲ.]

Wait a moment, please.

Зачекайте, будь ласка.
[zatʃɛ'kajtɛ, budʲ 'laska.]

Do you have any I.D.?

У вас є документи?
[u was 'ɛ doku'mɛnti?]

Thanks. You can leave now.

Дякую. Ви можете йти.
['dʲakuʲu. wi 'mɔʒɛtɛ jtɨ.]

Hands behind your head!

Руки за голову!
['ruki za 'hɔlowu!]

You're under arrest!

Ви заарештовані!
[wi zaarɛʃ'tɔwani!]

Health problems

Please help me.	**Допоможіть, будь ласка.** [dopomo'ʒitʲ, budʲ 'laska.]
I don't feel well.	**Мені погано.** [mɛ'ni po'ɦano.]
My husband doesn't feel well.	**Моєму чоловікові погано.** [mo'ɛmu ʧolo'wikowi po'ɦano.]
My son …	**Моєму сину …** [mo'ɛmu 'sinu …]
My father …	**Моєму батькові …** [mo'ɛmu 'batʲkowi …]

My wife doesn't feel well.	**Моїй дружині погано.** [mo'ij dru'ʒini po'ɦano.]
My daughter …	**Моїй дочці …** [mo'ij doʧ'ʦi …]
My mother …	**Моїй матері …** [mo'ij 'matɛri …]

I've got a …	**У мене болить …** [u 'mɛnɛ bo'litʲ …]
headache	**голова** [ɦolo'wa]
sore throat	**горло** ['ɦɔrlo]
stomach ache	**живіт** [ʒi'wit]
toothache	**зуб** [zub]

I feel dizzy.	**У мене паморочиться голова.** [u 'mɛnɛ 'pamoroʧitʲsʲa ɦolo'wa.]
He has a fever.	**У нього температура.** [u 'njɔɦo tɛmpɛra'tura.]
She has a fever.	**У неї температура.** [u nɛi tɛmpɛra'tura.]
I can't breathe.	**Я не можу дихати.** [ja nɛ 'mɔʒu 'dihatʲi.]

I'm short of breath.	**Я задихаюсь.** [ja zadi'haʲusʲ.]
I am asthmatic.	**Я астматик.** [ja ast'matik.]
I am diabetic.	**Я діабетик.** [ja dia'bɛtik.]

I can't sleep.

В мене безсоння.
[w 'mɛnɛ bɛz'sɔnʲa.]

food poisoning

харчове отруєння
[harʧo'wɛ ot'ruɛnʲa]

It hurts here.

Болить ось тут.
[bo'litʲ osʲ tut.]

Help me!

Допоможіть!
[dopomo'ʒitʲ!]

I am here!

Я тут!
[ja tut!]

We are here!

Ми тут!
[mɨ tut!]

Get me out of here!

Витягніть мене!
['witʲaɦnitʲ mɛ'nɛ!]

I need a doctor.

Мені потрібен лікар.
[mɛ'ni po'tribɛn 'likar.]

I can't move.

Я не можу рухатися.
[ja nɛ 'mɔʒu 'ruhatisʲa.]

I can't move my legs.

Я не відчуваю ніг.
[ja nɛ widʧu'waʲu niɦ.]

I have a wound.

Я поранений /поранена/.
[ja po'ranɛnij /po'ranɛna/.]

Is it serious?

Це серйозно?
[ʦɛ sɛr'jozno?]

My documents are in my pocket.

Мої документи в кишені.
[mo'i doku'mɛnti w ki'ʃɛni.]

Calm down!

Заспокойтеся!
[zaspo'kɔjtɛsʲa!]

May I use your phone?

Чи можна мені зателефонувати?
[ʧɨ 'mɔʒna mɛ'ni zatɛlɛfonu'wati?]

Call an ambulance!

Викличте швидку!
['wiklɨʧtɛ ʃwid'ku!]

It's urgent!

Це терміново!
[ʦɛ tɛrmi'nowo!]

It's an emergency!

Це дуже терміново!
[ʦɛ 'duʒɛ tɛrmi'nowo!]

Please hurry up!

Будь ласка, швидше!
[budʲ 'laska, 'ʃwidʲɛ!]

Would you please call a doctor?

Викличте лікаря, будь ласка.
['wiklɨʧtɛ 'likarʲa, budʲ 'laska.]

Where is the hospital?

Скажіть, де лікарня?
[ska'ʒitʲ, dɛ li'karnʲa?]

How are you feeling?

Як ви себе почуваєте?
[jak wɨ sɛ'bɛ poʧu'waɛtɛ?]

Are you all right?

З вами все гаразд?
[z 'wamɨ wsɛ ɦa'razd?]

What's happened?

Що трапилося?
[ɕo 'trapɨlosʲa?]

I feel better now.	**Мені вже краще.** [mɛ'ni wʒɛ 'kraɕɛ.]
It's OK.	**Все гаразд.** [wsɛ ɦa'razd.]
It's all right.	**Все добре.** [wsɛ 'dɔbrɛ.]

At the pharmacy

pharmacy (drugstore)	**аптека** [ap'tɛka]
24-hour pharmacy	**цілодобова аптека** [ʦilodo'bowa ap'tɛka]
Where is the closest pharmacy?	**Де найближча аптека?** [dɛ najb'liʒʧa ap'tɛka?]
Is it open now?	**Вона зараз відкрита?** [wo'na 'zaraz wid'krita?]
At what time does it open?	**О котрій вона відкривається?** [o kot'rij wo'na widkri'waɛt'sʲa?]
At what time does it close?	**До котрої години вона працює?** [do ko'trɔi ɦo'dini wo'na pra'ʦʲuɛ?]
Is it far?	**Це далеко?** [ʦɛ da'lɛko?]
Can I get there on foot?	**Я дійду туди пішки?** [ja dij'du tu'di 'piʃki?]
Can you show me on the map?	**Покажіть мені на карті, будь ласка.** [poka'ʒitʲ mɛ'ni na 'karti, budʲ 'laska.]
Please give me something for …	**Дайте мені, що-небудь від …** ['dajtɛ mɛ'ni, ɕo-'nɛbudʲ wid …]
a headache	**головного болю** [ɦolow'noɦo 'bɔlʲu]
a cough	**кашлю** ['kaʃlʲu]
a cold	**застуди** [za'studi]
the flu	**грипу** ['ɦripu]
a fever	**температури** [tɛmpɛra'turi]
a stomach ache	**болю в шлунку** ['bɔlʲu w 'ʃlunku]
nausea	**нудоти** [nu'dɔti]
diarrhea	**діареї** [dia'rɛi]
constipation	**запору** [za'pɔru]
pain in the back	**біль у спині** ['bilʲ u spi'ni]

chest pain	**біль у грудях** ['bilʲ u 'ɦrudʲah]
side stitch	**біль у боці** ['bilʲ u 'botsi]
abdominal pain	**біль в животі** ['bilʲ w ʒiwo'ti]

pill	**таблетка** [tab'lɛtka]
ointment, cream	**мазь, крем** [mazʲ, krɛm]
syrup	**сироп** [sɨ'rɔp]
spray	**спрей** ['sprɛj]
drops	**краплі** ['kraplі]

You need to go to the hospital.	**Вам потрібно в лікарню.** [wam po'tribno w li'karnʲu.]
health insurance	**страховка** [stra'hɔwka]
prescription	**рецепт** [rɛ'tsɛpt]
insect repellant	**засіб від комах** ['zasib wid ko'mah]
Band Aid	**лейкопластир** [lɛjko'plastir]

The bare minimum

Excuse me, ...
Вибачте, ...
['wɪbatʃtɛ, ...]

Hello.
Добрий день.
['dɔbrij dɛnʲ.]

Thank you.
Дякую.
['dʲakuʲu.]

Good bye.
До побачення.
[do po'batʃɛnʲa.]

Yes.
Так.
[tak.]

No.
Ні.
[ni.]

I don't know.
Я не знаю.
[ja nɛ 'znaʲu.]

Where? | Where to? | When?
Де? | Куди? | Коли?
[dɛ? | ku'dɪ? | ko'lɪ?]

I need ...
Мені потрібен ...
[mɛ'ni po'tribɛn ...]

I want ...
Я хочу ...
[ja 'hɔtʃu ...]

Do you have ...?
У вас є ...?
[u was 'ɛ ...?]

Is there a ... here?
Тут є ...?
[tut ɛ ...?]

May I ...?
Чи можна мені ...?
[tʃɪ 'mɔʒna mɛ'ni ...?]

..., please (polite request)
Будь ласка
[budʲ 'laska]

I'm looking for ...
Я шукаю ...
[ja ʃu'kaʲu ...]

restroom
туалет
[tua'lɛt]

ATM
банкомат
[banko'mat]

pharmacy (drugstore)
аптеку
[ap'tɛku]

hospital
лікарню
[li'karnʲu]

police station
поліцейську дільницю
[poli'tsɛjsʲku dilʲ'nɪtsʲu]

subway
метро
[mɛt'rɔ]

taxi	**таксі** [tak'si]
train station	**вокзал** [wok'zal]

My name is …	**Мене звуть …** [mɛ'nɛ zwutʲ …]
What's your name?	**Як вас звуть?** [jak was 'zwutʲ?]
Could you please help me?	**Допоможіть мені, будь ласка.** [dopomo'ʒitʲ mɛ'ni, budʲ 'laska.]
I've got a problem.	**У мене проблема.** [u 'mɛnɛ prob'lɛma.]
I don't feel well.	**Мені погано.** [mɛ'ni po'ɦano.]
Call an ambulance!	**Викличте швидку!** ['wiklitʃtɛ ʃwid'ku!]
May I make a call?	**Чи можна мені зателефонувати?** [tʃi 'mɔʒna mɛ'ni zatɛlɛfonu'wati?]

I'm sorry.	**Прошу вибачення** ['prɔʃu 'wibatʃɛnʲa]
You're welcome.	**Прошу** ['prɔʃu]

I, me	**я** [ja]
you (inform.)	**ти** [ti]
he	**він** [win]
she	**вона** [wo'na]
they (masc.)	**вони** [wo'ni]
they (fem.)	**вони** [wo'ni]
we	**ми** [mi]
you (pl)	**ви** [wi]
you (sg, form.)	**Ви** [wi]

ENTRANCE	**ВХІД** [whid]
EXIT	**ВИХІД** ['wihid]
OUT OF ORDER	**НЕ ПРАЦЮЄ** [nɛ pra'tsʲuɛ]
CLOSED	**ЗАКРИТО** [za'krito]

OPEN

ВІДКРИТО
[wid'krito]

FOR WOMEN

ДЛЯ ЖІНОК
[dlʲa ʒi'nɔk]

FOR MEN

ДЛЯ ЧОЛОВІКІВ
[dlʲa tʃolowi'kiw]

TOPICAL
VOCABULARY

This section contains more
than 3,000 of the most
important words.
The dictionary will provide
invaluable assistance while
traveling abroad, because
frequently individual words
are enough for you to be
understood.
The dictionary includes a
convenient transcription of
each foreign word

T&P Books Publishing

VOCABULARY
CONTENTS

T&P Books Publishing

BASIC CONCEPTS

T&P Books Publishing

1. Pronouns

I, me	я	[ja]
you	ти	[ti]
he	він	[win]
she	вона	[wo'na]
we	ми	[mi]
you (to a group)	ви	[wi]
they	вони	[wo'ni]

2. Greetings. Salutations

Hello! (fam.)	Здрастуй!	['zdrastuj]
Hello! (form.)	Здрастуйте!	['zdrastujtɛ]
Good morning!	Доброго ранку!	['dɔbroɦo 'ranku]
Good afternoon!	Добрий день!	['dɔbrij dɛnʲ]
Good evening!	Добрий вечір!	['dɔbrij 'wɛtʃir]
to say hello	вітатися	[wi'tatisʲa]
Hi! (hello)	Привіт!	[pri'wit]
greeting (n)	вітання (c)	[wi'tanʲa]
to greet (vt)	вітати	[wi'tati]
How are you?	Як справи?	[jak 'sprawi]
What's new?	Що нового?	[ɕo no'woɦo]
Bye-Bye! Goodbye!	До побачення!	[do po'batʃɛnʲa]
See you soon!	До швидкої зустрічі!	[do ʃwid'kɔji 'zustritʃi]
Farewell! (to a friend)	Прощавай!	[proɕa'waj]
Farewell! (form.)	Прощавайте!	[proɕa'wajtɛ]
to say goodbye	прощатися	[pro'ɕatisʲa]
So long!	Бувай!	[bu'waj]
Thank you!	Дякую!	['dʲakuʲu]
Thank you very much!	Щиро дякую!	['ɕiro 'dʲakuʲu]
You're welcome	Будь ласка.	[budʲ 'laska]
Don't mention it!	Не варто подяки	[nɛ 'warto po'dʲaki]
It was nothing	Нема за що.	[nɛ'ma za ɕo]
Excuse me! (fam.)	Вибач!	['wibatʃ]
Excuse me! (form.)	Вибачте!	['wibatʃtɛ]
to excuse (forgive)	вибачати	[wiba'tʃati]
to apologize (vi)	вибачатися	[wiba'tʃatisʲa]

My apologies	Моє вибачення.	[mo'ɛ 'wibatʃɛnʲa]
I'm sorry!	Вибачте!	['wibatʃtɛ]
to forgive (vt)	пробачати	[proba'tʃati]
please (adv)	будь ласка	[budʲ 'laska]

Don't forget!	Не забудьте!	[nɛ za'budʲtɛ]
Certainly!	Звичайно!	[zwi'tʃajno]
Of course not!	Звичайно ні!	[zwi'tʃajno ni]
Okay! (I agree)	Згоден!	['zɦɔdɛn]
That's enough!	Досить!	['dɔsitʲ]

3. Questions

Who?	Хто?	[hto]
What?	Що?	[ɕo]
Where? (at, in)	Де?	[dɛ]
Where (to)?	Куди?	[ku'di]
From where?	Звідки?	['zwidki]
When?	Коли?	[ko'li]
Why? (What for?)	Навіщо?	[na'wiɕo]
Why? (~ are you crying?)	Чому?	[tʃo'mu]

What for?	Для чого?	[dlʲa 'tʃɔɦo]
How? (in what way)	Як?	[jak]
What? (What kind of …?)	Який?	[ja'kij]
Which?	Котрий?	[kot'rij]

To whom?	Кому?	[ko'mu]
About whom?	Про кого?	[pro 'kɔɦo]
About what?	Про що?	[pro ɕo]
With whom?	З ким?	[z kim]

| How many? How much? | Скільки? | ['skilʲki] |
| Whose? | Чий? | [tʃij] |

4. Prepositions

with (accompanied by)	з	[z]
without	без	[bɛz]
to (indicating direction)	в	[w]
about (talking ~ …)	про	[pro]
before (in time)	перед	['pɛrɛd]
in front of …	перед	['pɛrɛd]

under (beneath, below)	під	[pid]
above (over)	над	[nad]
on (atop)	над	[nad]
from (off, out of)	з	[z]

of (made from)	з	[z]
in (e.g., ~ ten minutes)	за	[za]
over (across the top of)	через	['tʃɛrɛz]

5. Function words. Adverbs. Part 1

Where? (at, in)	Де?	[dɛ]
here (adv)	тут	[tut]
there (adv)	там	[tam]

| somewhere (to be) | десь | [dɛsʲ] |
| nowhere (not anywhere) | ніде | [ni'dɛ] |

| by (near, beside) | біля | ['bilʲa] |
| by the window | біля вікна | ['bilʲa wik'na] |

Where (to)?	Куди?	[ku'dɨ]
here (e.g., come ~!)	сюди	[sʲu'dɨ]
there (e.g., to go ~)	туди	[tu'dɨ]
from here (adv)	звідси	['zwidsɨ]
from there (adv)	звідти	['zwidtɨ]

| close (adv) | близько | ['blizʲko] |
| far (adv) | далеко | [da'lɛko] |

near (e.g., ~ Paris)	біля	['bilʲa]
nearby (adv)	поряд	['porʲad]
not far (adv)	недалеко	[nɛda'lɛko]

left (adj)	лівий	['liwɨj]
on the left	зліва	['zliwa]
to the left	ліворуч	[li'worutʃ]

right (adj)	правий	['prawɨj]
on the right	справа	['sprawa]
to the right	праворуч	[pra'worutʃ]

in front (adv)	спереду	['spɛrɛdu]
front (as adj)	передній	[pɛ'rɛdnij]
ahead (the kids ran ~)	уперед	[upɛ'rɛd]

behind (adv)	позаду	[po'zadu]
from behind	ззаду	['zzadu]
back (towards the rear)	назад	[na'zad]

| middle | середина (ж) | [sɛ'rɛdɨna] |
| in the middle | посередині | [posɛ'rɛdɨni] |

| at the side | збоку | ['zbɔku] |
| everywhere (adv) | скрізь | [skrizʲ] |

around (in all directions)	навколо	[naw'kɔlo]
from inside	зсередини	[zsɛ'rɛdini]
somewhere (to go)	кудись	[ku'disʲ]
straight (directly)	напрямки	[naprʲam'ki]
back (e.g., come ~)	назад	[na'zad]

| from anywhere | звідки-небудь | ['zwidki 'nɛbudʲ] |
| from somewhere | звідкись | ['zwidkisʲ] |

firstly (adv)	по-перше	[po 'pɛrʃɛ]
secondly (adv)	по-друге	[po 'druɦɛ]
thirdly (adv)	по-третє	[po t'rɛtɛ]

suddenly (adv)	раптом	['raptom]
at first (in the beginning)	спочатку	[spo'tʃatku]
for the first time	уперше	[u'pɛrʃɛ]
long before …	задовго до …	[za'dɔwɦo do]
anew (over again)	заново	['zanowo]
for good (adv)	назовсім	[na'zɔwsim]

never (adv)	ніколи	[ni'kɔli]
again (adv)	знову	['znɔwu]
now (adv)	тепер	[tɛ'pɛr]
often (adv)	часто	['tʃasto]
then (adv)	тоді	[to'di]
urgently (quickly)	терміново	[tɛrmi'nɔwo]
usually (adv)	звичайно	[zwi'tʃajno]

by the way, …	до речі	[do 'rɛtʃi]
possible (that is ~)	можливо	[moʒ'liwo]
probably (adv)	мабуть	[ma'butʲ]
maybe (adv)	може бути	['mɔʒɛ 'buti]
besides …	крім того, …	[krim 'tɔɦo]
that's why …	тому	[to'mu]
in spite of …	незважаючи на …	[nɛzwa'ʒaʲutʃi na]
thanks to …	завдяки …	[zawdʲa'ki]

what (pron.)	що	[ɕo]
that (conj.)	що	[ɕo]
something	щось	[ɕosʲ]
anything (something)	що-небудь	[ɕo 'nɛbudʲ]
nothing	нічого	[ni'tʃɔɦo]

who (pron.)	хто	[hto]
someone	хтось	[htosʲ]
somebody	хто-небудь	[hto 'nɛbudʲ]

nobody	ніхто	[nih'tɔ]
nowhere (a voyage to ~)	нікуди	['nikudi]
nobody's	нічий	[ni'tʃij]
somebody's	чий-небудь	[tʃij 'nɛbudʲ]
so (I'm ~ glad)	так	[tak]

also (as well)	також	[ta'kɔʒ]
too (as well)	також	[ta'kɔʒ]

6. Function words. Adverbs. Part 2

Why?	Чому?	[ʧo'mu]
for some reason	чомусь	[ʧo'musʲ]
because …	тому, що …	[to'mu, ɕo …]
for some purpose	навіщось	[na'wiɕosʲ]

and	і	[i]
or	або	[a'bɔ]
but	але	[a'lɛ]
for (e.g., ~ me)	для	[dlʲa]

too (~ many people)	занадто	[za'nadto]
only (exclusively)	тільки	['tilʲki]
exactly (adv)	точно	['tɔʧno]
about (more or less)	приблизно	[prib'lizno]

approximately (adv)	приблизно	[prib'lizno]
approximate (adj)	приблизний	[prib'liznij]
almost (adv)	майже	['majʒɛ]
the rest	решта (ж)	['rɛʃta]

each (adj)	кожен	['kɔʒɛn]
any (no matter which)	будь-який	[budʲ ja'kij]
many, much (a lot of)	багато	[ba'ɦato]
many people	багато хто	[ba'ɦato hto]
all (everyone)	всі	[wsi]

in return for …	в обмін на …	[w 'ɔbmin na]
in exchange (adv)	натомість	[na'tɔmistʲ]
by hand (made)	вручну	[wruʧ'nu]
hardly (negative opinion)	навряд чи	[naw'rʲad ʧi]

probably (adv)	мабуть	[ma'butʲ]
on purpose (intentionally)	навмисно	[naw'misno]
by accident (adv)	випадково	[wipad'kɔwo]

very (adv)	дуже	['duʒɛ]
for example (adv)	наприклад	[na'priklad]
between	між	[miʒ]
among	серед	['sɛrɛd]
so much (such a lot)	стільки	['stilʲki]
especially (adv)	особливо	[osob'liwo]

NUMBERS.
MISCELLANEOUS

T&P Books Publishing

7. Cardinal numbers. Part 1

0 zero	нуль	[nulʲ]
1 one	один	[o'din]
2 two	два	[dwa]
3 three	три	[tri]
4 four	чотири	[tʃo'tiri]
5 five	п'ять	[pʲʲatʲ]
6 six	шість	[ʃistʲ]
7 seven	сім	[sim]
8 eight	вісім	['wisim]
9 nine	дев'ять	['dɛwʲʲatʲ]
10 ten	десять	['dɛsʲatʲ]
11 eleven	одинадцять	[odi'nadtsʲatʲ]
12 twelve	дванадцять	[dwa'nadtsʲatʲ]
13 thirteen	тринадцять	[tri'nadtsʲatʲ]
14 fourteen	чотирнадцять	[tʃotir'nadtsʲatʲ]
15 fifteen	п'ятнадцять	[pʲʲat'nadtsʲatʲ]
16 sixteen	шістнадцять	[ʃist'nadtsʲatʲ]
17 seventeen	сімнадцять	[sim'nadtsʲatʲ]
18 eighteen	вісімнадцять	[wisim'nadtsʲatʲ]
19 nineteen	дев'ятнадцять	[dɛwʲʲat'nadtsʲatʲ]
20 twenty	двадцять	['dwadtsʲatʲ]
21 twenty-one	двадцять один	['dwadtsʲatʲ o'din]
22 twenty-two	двадцять два	['dwadtsʲatʲ dwa]
23 twenty-three	двадцять три	['dwadtsʲatʲ tri]
30 thirty	тридцять	['tridtsʲatʲ]
31 thirty-one	тридцять один	['tridtsʲatʲ o'din]
32 thirty-two	тридцять два	['tridtsʲatʲ dwa]
33 thirty-three	тридцять три	['tridtsʲatʲ tri]
40 forty	сорок	['sɔrok]
41 forty-one	сорок один	['sɔrok o'din]
42 forty-two	сорок два	['sɔrok dwa]
43 forty-three	сорок три	['sɔrok tri]
50 fifty	п'ятдесят	[pʲʲatdɛ'sʲat]
51 fifty-one	п'ятдесят один	[pʲʲatdɛ'sʲat o'din]
52 fifty-two	п'ятдесят два	[pʲʲatdɛ'sʲat dwa]
53 fifty-three	п'ятдесят три	[pʲʲatdɛ'sʲat tri]
60 sixty	шістдесят	[ʃizdɛ'sʲat]

61 sixty-one	шістдесят один	[ʃizdɛ'sʲat o'dɨn]
62 sixty-two	шістдесят два	[ʃizdɛ'sʲat dwa]
63 sixty-three	шістдесят три	[ʃizdɛ'sʲat trɨ]
70 seventy	сімдесят	[simdɛ'sʲat]
71 seventy-one	сімдесят один	[simdɛ'sʲat odɨn]
72 seventy-two	сімдесят два	[simdɛ'sʲat dwa]
73 seventy-three	сімдесят три	[simdɛ'sʲat trɨ]
80 eighty	вісімдесят	[wisimdɛ'sʲat]
81 eighty-one	вісімдесят один	[wisimdɛ'sʲat o'dɨn]
82 eighty-two	вісімдесят два	[wisimdɛ'sʲat dwa]
83 eighty-three	вісімдесят три	[wisimdɛ'sʲat trɨ]
90 ninety	дев'яносто	[dɛwʲa'nɔsto]
91 ninety-one	дев'яносто один	[dɛwʲa'nɔsto o'dɨn]
92 ninety-two	дев'яносто два	[dɛwʲa'nɔsto dwa]
93 ninety-three	дев'яносто три	[dɛwʲa'nɔsto trɨ]

8. Cardinal numbers. Part 2

100 one hundred	сто	[sto]
200 two hundred	двісті	['dwisti]
300 three hundred	триста	['trista]
400 four hundred	чотириста	[tʃo'tɨrista]
500 five hundred	п'ятсот	[pʲa'tsɔt]
600 six hundred	шістсот	[ʃist'sɔt]
700 seven hundred	сімсот	[sim'sɔt]
800 eight hundred	вісімсот	[wisim'sɔt]
900 nine hundred	дев'ятсот	[dɛwʲa'tsɔt]
1000 one thousand	тисяча	['tisʲatʃa]
2000 two thousand	дві тисячі	[dwi 'tisʲatʃi]
3000 three thousand	три тисячі	[trɨ 'tisʲatʃi]
10000 ten thousand	десять тисяч	['dɛsʲatʲ 'tisʲatʃ]
one hundred thousand	сто тисяч	[sto 'tisʲatʃ]
million	мільйон (ч)	[milʲ'jɔn]
billion	мільярд (ч)	[mi'ljard]

9. Ordinal numbers

first (adj)	перший	['pɛrʃɨj]
second (adj)	другий	['druɦɨj]
third (adj)	третій	['trɛtij]
fourth (adj)	четвертий	[tʃɛt'wɛrtɨj]
fifth (adj)	п'ятий	['pʲatɨj]
sixth (adj)	шостий	['ʃɔstɨj]

seventh (adj)	сьомий	['sʲɔmij]
eighth (adj)	восьмий	['wɔsʲmij]
ninth (adj)	дев'ятий	[dɛ'wʲjatij]
tenth (adj)	десятий	[dɛ'sʲatij]

COLOURS. UNITS OF MEASUREMENT

T&P Books Publishing

10. Colors

color	колір (ч)	['kɔlir]
shade (tint)	відтінок (ч)	[wid'tinok]
hue	тон (ч)	[ton]
rainbow	веселка (ж)	[wɛ'sɛlka]

white (adj)	білий	['biłij]
black (adj)	чорний	['tʃɔrnij]
gray (adj)	сірий	['sirij]

green (adj)	зелений	[zɛ'lɛnij]
yellow (adj)	жовтий	['ʒɔwtij]
red (adj)	червоний	[tʃɛr'wɔnij]
blue (adj)	синій	['sinij]
light blue (adj)	блакитний	[bla'kitnij]
pink (adj)	рожевий	[ro'ʒɛwij]
orange (adj)	помаранчевий	[poma'rantʃɛwij]
violet (adj)	фіолетовий	[fio'lɛtowij]
brown (adj)	коричневий	[ko'ritʃnɛwij]

golden (adj)	золотий	[zolo'tij]
silvery (adj)	сріблястий	[srib'łastij]
beige (adj)	бежевий	['bɛʒɛwij]
cream (adj)	кремовий	['krɛmowij]
turquoise (adj)	бірюзовий	[biru'zɔwij]
cherry red (adj)	вишневий	[wiʃ'nɛwij]
lilac (adj)	бузковий	[buz'kɔwij]
crimson (adj)	малиновий	[ma'łinowij]

light (adj)	світлий	['switłij]
dark (adj)	темний	['tɛmnij]
bright, vivid (adj)	яскравий	[jas'krawij]

colored (pencils)	кольоровий	[koło'rɔwij]
color (e.g., ~ film)	кольоровий	[koło'rɔwij]
black-and-white (adj)	чорно-білий	['tʃɔrno 'biłij]
plain (one-colored)	однобарвний	[odno'barwnij]
multicolored (adj)	різнобарвний	[rizno'barwnij]

11. Units of measurement

| weight | вага (ж) | [wa'ɦa] |
| length | довжина (ж) | [dowʒi'na] |

width	ширина (ж)	[ʃiri'na]
height	висота (ж)	[wiso'ta]
depth	глибина (ж)	[ɦlibi'na]
volume	об'єм (ч)	[o'bʲɛm]
area	площа (ж)	['plɔɕa]

gram	грам (ч)	[ɦram]
milligram	міліграм (ч)	[mili'ɦram]
kilogram	кілограм (ч)	[kilo'ɦram]
ton	тонна (ж)	['tɔna]
pound	фунт (ч)	['funt]
ounce	унція (ж)	['untsiʲa]

meter	метр (ч)	[mɛtr]
millimeter	міліметр (ч)	[mili'mɛtr]
centimeter	сантиметр (ч)	[santi'mɛtr]
kilometer	кілометр (ч)	[kilo'mɛtr]
mile	миля (ж)	['miʎʲa]

inch	дюйм (ч)	[dʲujm]
foot	фут (ч)	[fut]
yard	ярд (ч)	[jard]

square meter	квадратний метр (ч)	[kwad'ratnij mɛtr]
hectare	гектар (ч)	[ɦɛk'tar]
liter	літр (ч)	[litr]
degree	градус (ч)	['ɦradus]
volt	вольт (ч)	[wolʲt]
ampere	ампер (ч)	[am'pɛr]
horsepower	кінська сила (ж)	['kinsʲka 'siɫa]

quantity	кількість (ж)	['kiʎʲkistʲ]
a little bit of …	небагато …	[nɛba'ɦato]
half	половина (ж)	[polo'wina]
dozen	дюжина (ж)	['dʲuʒina]
piece (item)	штука (ж)	['ʃtuka]

size	розмір (ч)	['rɔzmir]
scale (map ~)	масштаб (ч)	[masʃ'tab]

minimal (adj)	мінімальний	[mini'maʎʲnij]
the smallest (adj)	найменший	[naj'mɛnʃij]
medium (adj)	середній	[sɛ'rɛdnij]
maximal (adj)	максимальний	[maksi'maʎʲnij]
the largest (adj)	найбільший	[naj'biʎʲʃij]

12. Containers

canning jar (glass ~)	банка (ж)	['banka]
can	банка (ж)	['banka]

| bucket | відро (с) | [wid'rɔ] |
| barrel | бочка (ж) | ['bɔtʃka] |

wash basin (e.g., plastic ~)	таз (ч)	[taz]
tank (100L water ~)	бак (ч)	[bak]
hip flask	фляжка (ж)	['flʲaʒka]
jerrycan	каністра (ж)	[ka'nistra]
tank (e.g., tank car)	цистерна (ж)	[tsis'tɛrna]

mug	кухоль (ч)	['kuholʲ]
cup (of coffee, etc.)	чашка (ж)	['tʃaʃka]
saucer	блюдце (с)	['blʲudtsɛ]
glass (tumbler)	склянка (ж)	['sklʲanka]
wine glass	келих (ч)	['kɛlih]
stock pot (soup pot)	каструля (ж)	[kas'trulʲa]

| bottle (~ of wine) | пляшка (ж) | ['plʲaʃka] |
| neck (of the bottle, etc.) | шийка (ж) | ['ʃijka] |

carafe (decanter)	карафа (ж)	[ka'rafa]
pitcher	глечик (ч)	['hlɛtʃik]
vessel (container)	посудина (ж)	[po'sudina]
pot (crock, stoneware ~)	горщик (ч)	['hɔrɕik]
vase	ваза (ж)	['waza]

bottle (perfume ~)	флакон (ч)	[fla'kɔn]
vial, small bottle	пляшечка (ж)	['plʲaʃɛtʃka]
tube (of toothpaste)	тюбик (ч)	['tʲubik]

sack (bag)	мішок (ч)	[mi'ʃɔk]
bag (paper ~, plastic ~)	пакет (ч)	[pa'kɛt]
pack (of cigarettes, etc.)	пачка (ж)	['patʃka]

box (e.g., shoebox)	коробка (ж)	[ko'rɔbka]
crate	ящик (ч)	['ʲaɕik]
basket	кошик (ч)	['kɔʃik]

MAIN VERBS

T&P Books Publishing

to advise (vt)	радити	['raditi]
to agree (say yes)	погоджуватися	[po'ɦɔdʒuwatisʲa]
to answer (vi, vt)	відповідати	[widpowi'dati]
to apologize (vi)	вибачатися	[wiba'tʃatisʲa]
to arrive (vi)	приїжджати	[priji'ʑati]

to ask (~ oneself)	запитувати	[za'pituwati]
to ask (~ sb to do sth)	просити	[pro'siti]
to be (vi)	бути	['buti]

to be afraid	боятися	[bo'ʲatisʲa]
to be hungry	хотіти їсти	[ho'titi 'jisti]
to be interested in …	цікавитися	[tsi'kawitisʲa]
to be needed	бути потрібним	['buti po'tribnim]
to be surprised	дивуватись	[diwu'watisʲ]

to be thirsty	хотіти пити	[ho'titi 'piti]
to begin (vt)	починати	[potʃi'nati]
to belong to …	належати	[na'lɛʒati]

| to boast (vi) | хвастатися | ['hwastatisʲa] |
| to break (split into pieces) | ламати | [la'mati] |

to call (~ for help)	кликати	['klikati]
can (v aux)	могти	[moɦ'ti]
to catch (vt)	ловити	[lo'witi]

| to change (vt) | поміняти | [pomi'nʲati] |
| to choose (select) | вибирати | [wibi'rati] |

to come down (the stairs)	спускатися	[spus'katisʲa]
to compare (vt)	зрівнювати	['zriwnʲuwati]
to complain (vi, vt)	скаржитися	['skarʒitisʲa]
to confuse (mix up)	помилятися	[pomi'lʲatisʲa]

| to continue (vt) | продовжувати | [pro'dɔwʒuwati] |
| to control (vt) | контролювати | [kontrolʲu'wati] |

to cook (dinner)	готувати	[ɦotu'wati]
to cost (vt)	коштувати	['kɔʃtuwati]
to count (add up)	лічити	[li'tʃiti]
to count on …	розраховувати на …	[rozra'ɦɔwuwati na]
to create (vt)	створити	[stwo'riti]
to cry (weep)	плакати	['plakati]

14. The most important verbs. Part 2

to deceive (vi, vt)	обманювати	[obˈmanʲuwati]
to decorate (tree, street)	прикрашати	[prikraˈʃati]
to defend (a country, etc.)	захищати	[zahiˈɕati]
to demand (request firmly)	вимагати	[wimaˈɦati]
to dig (vt)	рити	[ˈriti]

to discuss (vt)	обговорювати	[obɦoˈwɔrʲuwati]
to do (vt)	робити	[roˈbiti]
to doubt (have doubts)	сумніватися	[sumniˈwatisʲa]
to drop (let fall)	упускати	[upusˈkati]
to enter (room, house, etc.)	входити	[ˈwhɔditi]

to exist (vi)	існувати	[isnuˈwati]
to expect (foresee)	передбачити	[pɛrɛdˈbatʃiti]
to explain (vt)	пояснювати	[poˈʲasnʲuwati]
to fall (vi)	падати	[ˈpadati]
to find (vt)	знаходити	[znaˈhɔditi]
to finish (vt)	закінчувати	[zaˈkintʃuwati]
to fly (vi)	летіти	[lɛˈtiti]
to follow ... (come after)	іти слідом	[iˈti ˈslidom]
to forget (vi, vt)	забувати	[zabuˈwati]

to forgive (vt)	прощати	[proˈɕati]
to give (vt)	давати	[daˈwati]
to give a hint	натякати	[natʲaˈkati]
to go (on foot)	йти	[jti]
to go for a swim	купатися	[kuˈpatisʲa]
to go out (for dinner, etc.)	виходити	[wiˈhɔditi]
to guess (the answer)	відгадати	[widɦaˈdati]

to have (vt)	мати	[ˈmati]
to have breakfast	снідати	[ˈsnidati]
to have dinner	вечеряти	[wɛˈtʃɛrʲati]
to have lunch	обідати	[oˈbidati]
to hear (vt)	чути	[ˈtʃuti]

to help (vt)	допомагати	[dopomaˈɦati]
to hide (vt)	ховати	[hoˈwati]
to hope (vi, vt)	сподіватися	[spodiˈwatisʲa]
to hunt (vi, vt)	полювати	[polʲuˈwati]
to hurry (vi)	поспішати	[pospiˈʃati]

15. The most important verbs. Part 3

to inform (vt)	інформувати	[informuˈwati]
to insist (vi, vt)	наполягати	[napolʲaˈɦati]

to insult (vt)	ображати	[obra'ʒati]
to invite (vt)	запрошувати	[za'prɔʃuwati]
to joke (vi)	жартувати	[ʒartu'wati]

to keep (vt)	зберігати	[zbɛri'ɦati]
to keep silent	мовчати	[mow'tʃati]
to kill (vt)	убивати	[ubɨ'wati]
to know (sb)	знати	['znati]
to know (sth)	знати	['znati]
to laugh (vi)	сміятися	[smi'ʲatisʲa]

to liberate (city, etc.)	звільняти	[zwilʲ'nʲati]
to like (I like …)	подобатися	[po'dɔbatisʲa]
to look for … (search)	шукати	[ʃu'kati]
to love (sb)	кохати	[ko'ɦati]
to make a mistake	помилятися	[pomi'lʲatisʲa]

to manage, to run	керувати	[kɛru'wati]
to mean (signify)	означати	[ozna'tʃati]
to mention (talk about)	згадувати	['zɦaduwati]
to miss (school, etc.)	пропускати	[propus'kati]
to notice (see)	помічати	[pomi'tʃati]

to object (vi, vt)	заперечувати	[zapɛ'rɛtʃuwati]
to observe (see)	спостерігати	[spostɛri'ɦati]
to open (vt)	відчинити	[widtʃi'niti]
to order (meal, etc.)	замовляти	[zamow'lʲati]
to order (mil.)	наказувати	[na'kazuwati]
to own (possess)	володіти	[wolo'diti]

to participate (vi)	брати участь	['brati 'utʃastʲ]
to pay (vi, vt)	платити	[pla'titi]
to permit (vt)	дозволяти	[dozwo'lʲati]
to plan (vt)	планувати	[planu'wati]
to play (children)	грати	['ɦrati]

to pray (vi, vt)	молитися	[mo'litisʲa]
to prefer (vt)	воліти	[wo'liti]
to promise (vt)	обіцяти	[obi'tsʲati]
to pronounce (vt)	вимовляти	[wimow'lʲati]
to propose (vt)	пропонувати	[proponu'wati]
to punish (vt)	покарати	[poka'rati]

16. The most important verbs. Part 4

to read (vi, vt)	читати	[tʃi'tati]
to recommend (vt)	рекомендувати	[rɛkomɛndu'wati]
to refuse (vi, vt)	відмовлятися	[widmow'lʲatisʲa]
to regret (be sorry)	жалкувати	[ʒalku'wati]
to rent (sth from sb)	наймати	[naj'mati]

to repeat (say again)	повторювати	[pow'tɔrʲuwati]
to reserve, to book	резервувати	[rɛzɛrwu'wati]
to run (vi)	бігти	['biɦti]
to save (rescue)	рятувати	[rʲatu'wati]
to say (~ thank you)	сказати	[ska'zati]

to scold (vt)	лаяти	['laʲati]
to see (vt)	бачити	['batʃiti]
to sell (vt)	продавати	[proda'wati]
to send (vt)	відправляти	[widpraw'lʲati]
to shoot (vi)	стріляти	[stri'lʲati]

to shout (vi)	кричати	[kri'tʃati]
to show (vt)	показувати	[po'kazuwati]
to sign (document)	підписувати	[pid'pisuwati]
to sit down (vi)	сідати	[si'dati]

to smile (vi)	посміхатися	[posmi'hatisʲa]
to speak (vi, vt)	розмовляти	[rozmow'lʲati]
to steal (money, etc.)	красти	['krasti]
to stop (for pause, etc.)	зупинятися	[zupi'nʲatisʲa]
to stop (please ~ calling me)	припиняти	[pripi'nʲati]

to study (vt)	вивчати	[wiw'tʃati]
to swim (vi)	плавати	['plawati]
to take (vt)	брати	['brati]
to think (vi, vt)	думати	['dumati]
to threaten (vt)	погрожувати	[poɦ'rɔʒuwati]

to touch (with hands)	торкати	[tor'kati]
to translate (vt)	перекладати	[pɛrɛkla'dati]
to trust (vt)	довіряти	[dowi'rʲati]
to try (attempt)	пробувати	['prɔbuwati]
to turn (e.g., ~ left)	повертати	[powɛr'tati]

to underestimate (vt)	недооцінювати	[nɛdoo'tsinʲuwati]
to understand (vt)	розуміти	[rozu'miti]
to unite (vt)	об'єднувати	[o'bʲɛdnuwati]
to wait (vt)	чекати	[tʃɛ'kati]

to want (wish, desire)	хотіти	[ho'titi]
to warn (vt)	попереджувати	[popɛ'rɛdʒuwati]
to work (vi)	працювати	[pratsʲu'wati]
to write (vt)	писати	[pi'sati]
to write down	записувати	[za'pisuwati]

TIME. CALENDAR

T&P Books Publishing

17. Weekdays

Monday	понеділок (ч)	[ponɛ'dilok]
Tuesday	вівторок (ч)	[wiw'tɔrok]
Wednesday	середа (ж)	[sɛrɛ'da]
Thursday	четвер (ч)	[tʃɛt'wɛr]
Friday	п'ятниця (ж)	['pʲatnitsʲa]
Saturday	субота (ж)	[su'bɔta]
Sunday	неділя (ж)	[nɛ'dilʲa]

today (adv)	сьогодні	[sʲo'hɔdni]
tomorrow (adv)	завтра	['zawtra]
the day after tomorrow	післязавтра	[pislʲa'zawtra]
yesterday (adv)	вчора	['wtʃora]
the day before yesterday	позавчора	[pozaw'tʃora]

day	день (ч)	[dɛnʲ]
working day	робочий день (ч)	[ro'botʃij dɛnʲ]
public holiday	святковий день (ч)	[swʲat'kɔwij dɛnʲ]
day off	вихідний день (ч)	[wihid'nij dɛnʲ]
weekend	вихідні (мн)	[wihid'ni]

all day long	весь день	[wɛsʲ dɛnʲ]
the next day (adv)	на наступний день	[na na'stupnij dɛnʲ]
two days ago	2 дні тому	[dwa dni 'tɔmu]
the day before	напередодні	[napɛrɛ'dɔdni]
daily (adj)	щоденний	[ɕo'dɛnij]
every day (adv)	щодня	[ɕod'nʲa]

week	тиждень (ч)	['tiʒdɛnʲ]
last week (adv)	на минулому тижні	[na mi'nulomu 'tiʒni]
next week (adv)	на наступному тижні	[na na'stupnomu 'tiʒni]
weekly (adj)	щотижневий	[ɕotiʒ'nɛwij]
every week (adv)	щотижня	[ɕo'tiʒnʲa]
twice a week	два рази на тиждень	[dwa 'razi na 'tiʒdɛnʲ]
every Tuesday	кожен вівторок	['kɔʒɛn wiw'tɔrok]

18. Hours. Day and night

morning	ранок (ч)	['ranok]
in the morning	вранці	['wrantsi]
noon, midday	полудень (ч)	['poludɛnʲ]
in the afternoon	після обіду	['pislʲa o'bidu]
evening	вечір (ч)	['wɛtʃir]

in the evening	увечері	[u'wɛtʃɛri]
night	ніч (ж)	[nitʃ]
at night	уночі	[uno'tʃi]
midnight	північ (ж)	['piwnitʃ]

second	секунда (ж)	[sɛ'kunda]
minute	хвилина (ж)	[hwi'lina]
hour	година (ж)	[ɦo'dina]
half an hour	півгодини (мн)	[piwɦo'dini]
a quarter-hour	чверть (ж) години	[tʃwɛrtʲ ɦo'dini]
fifteen minutes	15 хвилин	[pʲat'nadtsʲatʲ hwi'lin]
24 hours	доба (ж)	[do'ba]

sunrise	схід (ч) сонця	[shid 'sɔntsʲa]
dawn	світанок (ч)	[swi'tanok]
early morning	ранній ранок (ч)	['ranij 'ranok]
sunset	захід (ч)	['zahid]

early in the morning	рано вранці	['rano 'wrantsi]
this morning	сьогодні вранці	[sʲo'ɦodni 'wrantsi]
tomorrow morning	завтра вранці	['zawtra 'wrantsi]

this afternoon	сьогодні вдень	[sʲo'ɦodni wdɛnʲ]
in the afternoon	після обіду	['pislʲa o'bidu]
tomorrow afternoon	завтра після обіду (ч)	['zawtra 'pislʲa o'bidu]

| tonight (this evening) | сьогодні увечері | [sʲo'ɦodni u'wɛtʃɛri] |
| tomorrow night | завтра увечері | ['zawtra u'wɛtʃɛri] |

at 3 o'clock sharp	рівно о третій годині	['riwno o t'rɛtij ɦo'dini]
about 4 o'clock	біля четвертої години	['bilʲa tʃɛt'wɛrtoji ɦo'dini]
by 12 o'clock	до дванадцятої години	[do dwa'nadtsʲatoji ɦo'dini]

in 20 minutes	за двадцять хвилин	[za 'dwadtsʲatʲ hwi'lin]
in an hour	за годину	[za ɦo'dinu]
on time (adv)	вчасно	['wtʃasno]

a quarter of …	без чверті	[bɛz 'tʃwɛrti]
within an hour	на протязі години	[na 'prɔtʲazi ɦo'dini]
every 15 minutes	що п'ятнадцять хвилин	[ɕo pʲat'nadtsʲatʲ hwi'lin]
round the clock	цілодобово	[tsilodo'bɔwo]

19. Months. Seasons

January	січень (ч)	['sitʃɛnʲ]
February	лютий (ч)	['lʲutij]
March	березень (ч)	['bɛrɛzɛnʲ]
April	квітень (ч)	['kwitɛnʲ]
May	травень (ч)	['trawɛnʲ]
June	червень (ч)	['tʃɛrwɛnʲ]

July	**липень** (ч)	['lipɛnʲ]
August	**серпень** (ч)	['sɛrpɛnʲ]
September	**вересень** (ч)	['wɛrɛsɛnʲ]
October	**жовтень** (ч)	['ʒɔwtɛnʲ]
November	**листопад** (ч)	[listo'pad]
December	**грудень** (ч)	['ɦrudɛnʲ]

spring	**весна** (ж)	[wɛs'na]
in spring	**навесні**	[nawɛs'ni]
spring (as adj)	**весняний**	[wɛs'nʲanij]

summer	**літо** (с)	['lito]
in summer	**влітку**	['wlitku]
summer (as adj)	**літній**	['litnij]

fall	**осінь** (ж)	['ɔsinʲ]
in fall	**восени**	[wosɛ'ni]
fall (as adj)	**осінній**	[o'sinij]

winter	**зима** (ж)	[zi'ma]
in winter	**взимку**	['wzimku]
winter (as adj)	**зимовий**	[zi'mɔwij]

month	**місяць** (ч)	['misʲats]
this month	**в цьому місяці** (ч)	[w tsʲomu 'misʲatsi]
next month	**в наступному місяці** (ч)	[w na'stupnomu 'misʲatsi]
last month	**в минулому місяці** (ч)	[w mɨ'nulomu 'misʲatsi]

a month ago	**місяць** (ч) **тому**	['misʲats to'mu]
in a month (a month later)	**через місяць**	['tʃɛrɛz 'misʲats]
in 2 months (2 months later)	**через 2 місяці**	['tʃɛrɛz dwa 'misʲatsi]
the whole month	**весь місяць** (ч)	[wɛsʲ 'misʲats]
all month long	**цілий місяць**	['tsilij 'misʲats]

monthly (~ magazine)	**щомісячний**	[ɕo'misʲatʃnij]
monthly (adv)	**щомісяця**	[ɕo'misʲatsʲa]
every month	**кожний місяць** (ч)	['kɔʒnij 'misʲats]
twice a month	**два рази на місяць**	[dwa 'razi na 'misʲats]

year	**рік** (ч)	[rik]
this year	**в цьому році**	[w tsʲomu 'rɔtsi]
next year	**в наступному році**	[w na'stupnomu 'rɔtsi]
last year	**в минулому році**	[w mɨ'nulomu 'rɔtsi]

a year ago	**рік тому**	[rik 'tomu]
in a year	**через рік**	['tʃɛrɛz rik]
in two years	**через два роки**	['tʃɛrɛz dwa 'rɔki]
the whole year	**увесь рік**	[u'wɛsʲ rik]
all year long	**цілий рік**	['tsilij rik]
every year	**кожен рік**	['kɔʒɛn 'rik]
annual (adj)	**щорічний**	[ɕo'ritʃnij]

annually (adv)	**щороку**	[ɕo'rɔku]
4 times a year	**чотири рази на рік**	[ʧo'tiri 'razɨ na rik]
date (e.g., today's ~)	**число** (c)	[ʧis'lɔ]
date (e.g., ~ of birth)	**дата** (ж)	['data]
calendar	**календар** (ч)	[kalɛn'dar]
half a year	**півроку**	[piw'rɔku]
six months	**півріччя** (c)	[piw'riʧʲa]
season (summer, etc.)	**сезон** (ч)	[sɛ'zɔn]
century	**вік** (ч)	[wik]

TRAVEL. HOTEL

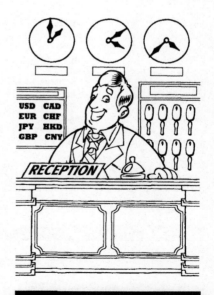

T&P Books Publishing

20. Trip. Travel

tourism, travel	туризм (ч)	[tu'rizm]
tourist	турист (ч)	[tu'rist]
trip, voyage	мандрівка (ж)	[mand'riwka]
adventure	пригода (ж)	[pri'ɦɔda]
trip, journey	поїздка (ж)	[po'jizdka]
vacation	відпустка (ж)	[wid'pustka]
to be on vacation	бути у відпустці	['butɨ u wid'pusttsi]
rest	відпочинок (ч)	[widpo'tʃinok]
train	поїзд (ч)	['pɔjizd]
by train	поїздом	['pɔjizdom]
airplane	літак (ч)	[li'tak]
by airplane	літаком	[lita'kɔm]
by car	автомобілем	[awtomo'bilɛm]
by ship	кораблем	[korab'lɛm]
luggage	багаж (ч)	[ba'ɦaʒ]
suitcase	валіза (ж)	[wa'liza]
luggage cart	візок (ч) для багажу	[wi'zɔk dlʲa baɦa'ʒu]
passport	паспорт (ч)	['pasport]
visa	віза (ж)	['wiza]
ticket	квиток (ч)	[kwi'tɔk]
air ticket	авіаквиток (ч)	[awiakwi'tɔk]
guidebook	путівник (ч)	[putiw'nik]
map (tourist ~)	карта (ж)	['karta]
area (rural ~)	місцевість (ж)	[mis'tsɛwistʲ]
place, site	місце (с)	['mistsɛ]
exotica (n)	екзотика (ж)	[ɛk'zɔtika]
exotic (adj)	екзотичний	[ɛkzo'titʃnij]
amazing (adj)	дивовижний	['diwowiʒnij]
group	група (ж)	['ɦrupa]
excursion, sightseeing tour	екскурсія (ж)	[ɛks'kursiʲa]
guide (person)	екскурсовод (ч)	[ɛkskurso'wɔd]

21. Hotel

hotel	готель (ч)	[ɦo'tɛlʲ]
motel	мотель (ч)	[mo'tɛlʲ]

three-star (~ hotel)	три зірки	[tri 'zirki]
five-star	п'ять зірок	[pʲatʲ zi'rɔk]
to stay (in a hotel, etc.)	зупинитися	[zupi'nitisʲa]

room	номер (ч)	['nɔmɛr]
single room	одномісний номер (ч)	[odno'misnij nomɛr]
double room	двомісний номер (ч)	[dwo'misnij 'nɔmɛr]
to book a room	резервувати номер	[rɛzɛrwu'wati 'nɔmɛr]

| half board | напівпансіон (ч) | [napiwpansi'ɔn] |
| full board | повний пансіон (ч) | ['pɔwnij pansi'ɔn] |

with bath	з ванною	[z 'wanoʲu]
with shower	з душем	[z 'duʃɛm]
satellite television	супутникове телебачення (с)	[su'putnikowɛ tɛlɛ'batʃɛnʲa]
air-conditioner	кондиціонер (ч)	[konditsio'nɛr]
towel	рушник (ч)	[ruʃ'nik]
key	ключ (ч)	[klʲutʃ]

administrator	адміністратор (ч)	[admini'strator]
chambermaid	покоївка (ж)	[poko'jiwka]
porter, bellboy	носильник (ч)	[no'silʲnik]
doorman	портьє (ч)	[por'tʲɛ]

restaurant	ресторан (ч)	[rɛsto'ran]
pub, bar	бар (ч)	[bar]
breakfast	сніданок (ч)	[sni'danok]
dinner	вечеря (ж)	[wɛ'tʃɛrʲa]
buffet	шведський стіл (ч)	['ʃwɛdsʲkij stil]

| lobby | вестибюль (ч) | [wɛsti'bʲulʲ] |
| elevator | ліфт (ч) | [lift] |

| DO NOT DISTURB | НЕ ТУРБУВАТИ | [nɛ turbu'wati] |
| NO SMOKING | ПАЛИТИ ЗАБОРОНЕНО | [pa'liti zabo'rɔnɛno] |

22. Sightseeing

monument	пам'ятник (ч)	['pamʲatnik]
fortress	фортеця (ж)	[for'tɛtsʲa]
palace	палац (ч)	[pa'lats]
castle	замок (ч)	['zamok]
tower	вежа (ж)	['wɛʒa]
mausoleum	мавзолей (ч)	[mawzo'lɛj]

architecture	архітектура (ж)	[arhitɛk'tura]
medieval (adj)	середньовічний	[sɛrɛdnʲo'witʃnij]
ancient (adj)	старовинний	[staro'winij]
national (adj)	національний	[natsio'nalʲnij]

famous (monument, etc.)	**відомий**	[wi'dɔmij]
tourist	**турист** (ч)	[tu'rist]
guide (person)	**гід** (ч)	[hid]
excursion, sightseeing tour	**екскурсія** (ж)	[ɛks'kursiʲa]
to show (vt)	**показувати**	[po'kazuwati]
to tell (vt)	**розповідати**	[rozpowi'dati]
to find (vt)	**знайти**	[znaj'ti]
to get lost (lose one's way)	**загубитися**	[zaɦu'bitisʲa]
map (e.g., subway ~)	**схема** (ж)	['sɦɛma]
map (e.g., city ~)	**план** (ч)	[plan]
souvenir, gift	**сувенір** (ч)	[suwɛ'nir]
gift shop	**магазин** (ч) **сувенірів**	[maɦa'zin suwɛ'niriw]
to take pictures	**фотографувати**	[fotoɦrafu'wati]
to have one's picture taken	**фотографуватися**	[fotoɦrafu'watisʲa]

TRANSPORTATION

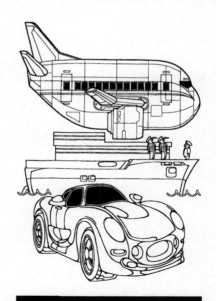

23. Airport

airport	аеропорт (ч)	[aɛro'pɔrt]
airplane	літак (ч)	[li'tak]
airline	авіакомпанія (ж)	[awiakom'paniʲa]
air traffic controller	диспетчер (ч)	[dɨs'pɛʧɛr]

departure	виліт (ч)	['wɨlit]
arrival	приліт (ч)	[pri'lit]
to arrive (by plane)	прилетіти	[pri'lɛtiti]

| departure time | час (ч) вильоту | [ʧas 'wɨlʲotu] |
| arrival time | час (ч) прильоту | [ʧas prilʲotu] |

| to be delayed | затримуватися | [za'trimuwatisʲa] |
| flight delay | затримка (ж) вильоту | [za'trimka 'wɨlʲotu] |

information board	інформаційне табло (с)	[informa'ʦijnɛ tab'lɔ]
information	інформація (ж)	[infor'matsiʲa]
to announce (vt)	оголошувати	[oɦo'lɔʃuwati]
flight (e.g., next ~)	рейс (ч)	[rɛjs]

| customs | митниця (ж) | ['mitnɨʦʲa] |
| customs officer | митник (ч) | ['mitnik] |

customs declaration	декларація (ж)	[dɛkla'ratsiʲa]
to fill out (vt)	заповнити	[za'powniti]
to fill out the declaration	заповнити декларацію	[za'powniti dɛkla'ratsiʲu]
passport control	паспортний контроль (ч)	['pasportnij kon'trolʲ]

luggage	багаж (ч)	[ba'ɦaʒ]
hand luggage	ручний вантаж (ж)	[ruʧ'nij wan'taʒ]
luggage cart	візок (ч) для багажу	[wi'zɔk dlʲa baɦa'ʒu]

landing	посадка (ж)	[po'sadka]
landing strip	посадкова смуга (ж)	[po'sadkowa 'smuɦa]
to land (vi)	сідати	[si'dati]
airstairs	трап (ч)	[trap]

check-in	реєстрація (ж)	[rɛɛ'stratsiʲa]
check-in counter	реєстрація (ж)	[rɛɛ'stratsiʲa]
to check-in (vi)	зареєструватися	[zarɛɛstru'watisʲa]
boarding pass	посадковий талон (ч)	[po'sadkowij ta'lɔn]
departure gate	вихід (ч)	['wɨhid]
transit	транзит (ч)	[tran'zit]

to wait (vi)	чекати	[tʃɛ'kati]
departure lounge	зал (ч) очікування	['zal o'tʃikuwanʲa]
to see off	проводжати	[prowo'dʒati]
to say goodbye	прощатися	[pro'ɕatisʲa]

24. Airplane

airplane	літак (ч)	[li'tak]
air ticket	авіаквиток (ч)	[awiakwi'tɔk]
airline	авіакомпанія (ж)	[awiakom'panʲa]
airport	аеропорт (ч)	[aɛro'pɔrt]
supersonic (adj)	надзвуковий	[nadzwuko'wij]

captain	командир (ч) корабля	[koman'dir korab'lʲa]
crew	екіпаж (ч)	[ɛki'paʒ]
pilot	пілот (ч)	[pi'lɔt]
flight attendant (fem.)	стюардеса (ж)	[stʲuar'dɛsa]
navigator	штурман (ч)	['ʃturman]

wings	крила (мн)	['krila]
tail	хвіст (ч)	[hwist]
cockpit	кабіна (ж)	[ka'bina]
engine	двигун (ч)	[dwi'ɦun]
undercarriage (landing gear)	шасі (с)	[ʃa'si]
turbine	турбіна (ж)	[tur'bina]

propeller	пропелер (ч)	[pro'pɛlɛr]
black box	чорна скринька (ж)	['tʃɔrna 'skrinʲka]
yoke (control column)	штурвал (ч)	[ʃtur'wal]
fuel	пальне (с)	[palʲ'nɛ]

safety card	інструкція (ж)	[inst'ruktsiʲa]
oxygen mask	киснева маска (ж)	['kisnɛwa 'maska]
uniform	уніформа (ж)	[uni'fɔrma]
life vest	рятувальний жилет (ч)	[rʲatu'walʲnij ʒi'lɛt]
parachute	парашут (ч)	[para'ʃut]

takeoff	зліт (ч)	[zlit]
to take off (vi)	злітати	[zli'tati]
runway	злітна смуга (ж)	['zlitna 'smuɦa]

visibility	видимість (ж)	['widimistʲ]
flight (act of flying)	політ (ч)	[po'lit]
altitude	висота (ж)	[wiso'ta]
air pocket	повітряна яма (ж)	[po'witrʲana 'jama]

seat	місце (с)	['mistsɛ]
headphones	навушники (мн)	[na'wuʃniki]
folding tray (tray table)	відкидний столик (ч)	[widkɪd'nij 'stɔlik]

| airplane window | ілюмінатор (ч) | [iljumiˈnator] |
| aisle | прохід (ч) | [proˈhid] |

25. Train

train	поїзд (ч)	[ˈpɔjizd]
commuter train	електропоїзд (ч)	[ɛlɛktroˈpɔjizd]
express train	швидкий поїзд (ч)	[ʃwidˈkij ˈpɔjizd]
diesel locomotive	тепловоз (ч)	[tɛploˈwɔz]
steam locomotive	паровоз (ч)	[paroˈwɔz]

| passenger car | вагон (ч) | [waˈhɔn] |
| dining car | вагон-ресторан (ч) | [waˈhɔn rɛstoˈran] |

rails	рейки (мн)	[ˈrɛjki]
railroad	залізниця (ж)	[zalizˈnitsʲa]
railway tie	шпала (ж)	[ˈʃpala]

platform (railway ~)	платформа (ж)	[platˈfɔrma]
track (~ 1, 2, etc.)	колія (ж)	[ˈkɔliʲa]
semaphore	семафор (ч)	[sɛmaˈfɔr]
station	станція (ж)	[ˈstantsiʲa]

engineer (train driver)	машиніст (ч)	[maʃiˈnist]
porter (of luggage)	носильник (ч)	[noˈsilʲnik]
car attendant	провідник (ч)	[prowidˈnik]
passenger	пасажир (ч)	[pasaˈʒir]
conductor	контролер (ч)	[kontroˈlɛr]
(ticket inspector)		

| corridor (in train) | коридор (ч) | [koriˈdɔr] |
| emergency brake | стоп-кран (ч) | [stop kran] |

compartment	купе (с)	[kuˈpɛ]
berth	полиця (ж)	[poˈlitsʲa]
upper berth	полиця (ж) верхня	[poˈlitsʲa ˈwɛrhnʲa]
lower berth	полиця (ж) нижня	[poˈlitsʲa ˈniʒnʲa]
bed linen, bedding	білизна (ж)	[biˈlizna]

ticket	квиток (ч)	[kwiˈtɔk]
schedule	розклад (ч)	[ˈrɔzklad]
information display	табло (с)	[tabˈlɔ]

to leave, to depart	відходити	[widˈhɔditi]
departure (of train)	відправлення (с)	[widˈprawlɛnʲa]
to arrive (ab. train)	прибувати	[pribuˈwati]
arrival	прибуття (с)	[pributˈtʲa]

| to arrive by train | приїхати поїздом | [priˈjihati ˈpɔjizdom] |
| to get on the train | сісти на поїзд | [ˈsisti na ˈpɔjizd] |

to get off the train	зійти з поїзду	[zij'ti z 'pojizdu]
train wreck	катастрофа (ж)	[kata'strɔfa]
steam locomotive	паровоз (ч)	[paro'wɔz]
stoker, fireman	кочегар (ч)	[kotʃɛ'ɦar]
firebox	топка (ж)	['tɔpka]
coal	вугілля (с)	[wu'ɦilʲa]

26. Ship

| ship | корабель (ч) | [kora'bɛlʲ] |
| vessel | судно (с) | ['sudno] |

steamship	пароплав (ч)	[paro'plaw]
riverboat	теплохід (ч)	[tɛplo'hid]
cruise ship	лайнер (ч)	['lajnɛr]
cruiser	крейсер (ч)	['krɛjsɛr]

yacht	яхта (ж)	['ʲahta]
tugboat	буксир (ч)	[buk'sir]
barge	баржа (ж)	['barʒa]
ferry	паром (ч)	[pa'rɔm]

| sailing ship | вітрильник (ч) | [wi'trilʲnik] |
| brigantine | бригантина (ж) | [briɦan'tina] |

| ice breaker | криголам (ч) | [kriɦo'lam] |
| submarine | човен (ч) підводний | ['tʃɔwɛn pid'wɔdnij] |

boat (flat-bottomed ~)	човен (ч)	['tʃɔwɛn]
dinghy	шлюпка (ж)	['ʃlʲupka]
lifeboat	шлюпка (ж) рятувальна	['ʃlʲupka rʲatu'walʲna]
motorboat	катер (ч)	['katɛr]

captain	капітан (ч)	[kapi'tan]
seaman	матрос (ч)	[mat'rɔs]
sailor	моряк (ч)	[mo'rʲak]
crew	екіпаж (ч)	[ɛki'paʒ]

boatswain	боцман (ч)	['bɔtsman]
ship's boy	юнга (ч)	['ʲunɦa]
cook	кок (ч)	[kok]
ship's doctor	судновий лікар (ч)	['sudnowij 'likar]

deck	палуба (ж)	['paluba]
mast	щогла (ж)	['ɕɔɦla]
sail	вітрило (с)	[wi'trilo]

hold	трюм (ч)	[trʲum]
bow (prow)	ніс (ч)	[nis]
stern	корма (ж)	[kor'ma]

oar	весло (с)	[wɛsˈlɔ]
screw propeller	гвинт (ч)	[ɦwint]
cabin	каюта (ж)	[kaˈʲuta]
wardroom	кают-компанія (ж)	[kaˈʲut komˈpaniʲa]
engine room	машинне відділення (с)	[maˈʃinɛ widˈdilɛnʲa]
bridge	капітанський місток (ч)	[kapiˈtansʲkij misˈtɔk]
radio room	радіорубка (ж)	[radioˈrubka]
wave (radio)	хвиля (ж)	[ˈhwiʎa]
logbook	судновий журнал (ч)	[ˈsudnowij ʒurˈnal]
spyglass	підзорна труба (ж)	[piˈdzɔrna truˈba]
bell	дзвін (ч)	[dzwin]
flag	прапор (ч)	[ˈprapor]
hawser (mooring ~)	канат (ч)	[kaˈnat]
knot (bowline, etc.)	вузол (ч)	[ˈwuzol]
deckrails	поручень (ч)	[ˈpɔrutʃɛnʲ]
gangway	трап (ч)	[trap]
anchor	якір (ч)	[ˈʲakir]
to weigh anchor	підняти якір	[pidˈnʲati ˈjakir]
to drop anchor	кинути якір	[ˈkinuti ˈjakir]
anchor chain	якірний ланцюг (ч)	[ˈʲakirnij lanˈtsʲuɦ]
port (harbor)	порт (ч)	[port]
quay, wharf	причал (ч)	[priˈtʃal]
to berth (moor)	причалювати	[priˈtʃalʲuwati]
to cast off	відчалювати	[widˈtʃalʲuwati]
trip, voyage	подорож (ж)	[ˈpɔdorɔʒ]
cruise (sea trip)	круїз (ч)	[kruˈjiz]
course (route)	курс (ч)	[kurs]
route (itinerary)	маршрут (ч)	[marˈʃrut]
fairway	фарватер (ч)	[farˈwatɛr]
(safe water channel)		
shallows	мілина (ж)	[miliˈna]
to run aground	сісти на мілину	[ˈsisti na miliˈnu]
storm	буря (ж)	[ˈburʲa]
signal	сигнал (ч)	[siɦˈnal]
to sink (vi)	тонути	[toˈnuti]
SOS (distress signal)	SOS	[sos]
ring buoy	рятувальний круг (ч)	[rʲatuˈwalʲnij ˈkruɦ]

CITY

T&P Books Publishing

27. Urban transportation

bus	автобус (ч)	[aw'tɔbus]
streetcar	трамвай (ч)	[tram'waj]
trolley bus	тролейбус (ч)	[tro'lɛjbus]
route (of bus, etc.)	маршрут (ч)	[marʃ'rut]
number (e.g., bus ~)	номер (ч)	['nɔmɛr]

to go by ...	їхати на ...	['jihatɨ na]
to get on (~ the bus)	сісти	['sistɨ]
to get off ...	зійти	[zij'tɨ]

stop (e.g., bus ~)	зупинка (ж)	[zu'pɨnka]
next stop	наступна зупинка (ж)	[na'stupna zu'pɨnka]
terminus	кінцева зупинка (ж)	[kin'tsɛwa zu'pɨnka]
schedule	розклад (ч)	['rɔzklad]
to wait (vt)	чекати	[ʧɛ'katɨ]

| ticket | квиток (ч) | [kwɨ'tɔk] |
| fare | вартість (ж) квитка | ['wartistʲ kwɨt'ka] |

cashier (ticket seller)	касир (ч)	[ka'sɨr]
ticket inspection	контроль (ч)	[kon'trɔlʲ]
ticket inspector	контролер (ч)	[kontro'lɛr]

to be late (for ...)	запізнюватися	[za'piznʲuwatisʲa]
to miss (~ the train, etc.)	спізнитися	[spiz'nitisʲa]
to be in a hurry	поспішати	[pospi'ʃatɨ]

taxi, cab	таксі (с)	[tak'si]
taxi driver	таксист (ч)	[tak'sɨst]
by taxi	на таксі	[na tak'si]
taxi stand	стоянка (с) таксі	[stoˈjanka tak'si]
to call a taxi	викликати таксі	['wɨklɨkatɨ tak'si]
to take a taxi	взяти таксі	['wzʲatɨ tak'si]

traffic	вуличний рух (ч)	['wulɨʧnɨj ruh]
traffic jam	пробка (ж)	['prɔbka]
rush hour	години (мн) пік	[ɦo'dɨnɨ pik]
to park (vi)	паркуватися	[parku'watisʲa]
to park (vt)	паркувати	[parku'watɨ]
parking lot	стоянка (ж)	[stoˈjanka]

subway	метро (с)	[mɛt'rɔ]
station	станція (ж)	['stantsiʲa]
to take the subway	їхати в метро	['jihatɨ w mɛt'rɔ]

| train | поїзд (ч) | ['pɔjizd] |
| train station | вокзал (ч) | [wok'zal] |

28. City. Life in the city

city, town	місто (с)	['misto]
capital city	столиця (ж)	[sto'litsʲa]
village	село (с)	[sɛ'lɔ]

city map	план (ч) міста	[plan 'mista]
downtown	центр (ч) міста	[tsɛntr 'mista]
suburb	передмістя (с)	[pɛrɛd'mistʲa]
suburban (adj)	приміський	[primisʲ'kij]

outskirts	околиця (ж)	[o'kɔlitsʲa]
environs (suburbs)	околиці (мн)	[o'kɔlitsi]
city block	квартал (ч)	[kwar'tal]
residential block (area)	житловий квартал (ч)	[ʒitlo'wij kwar'tal]

traffic	рух (ч)	[ruh]
traffic lights	світлофор (ч)	[switlo'fɔr]
public transportation	міський транспорт (ч)	[misʲ'kij 'transport]
intersection	перехрестя (с)	[pɛrɛh'rɛstʲa]

crosswalk	перехід (ч)	[pɛrɛ'hid]
pedestrian underpass	підземний перехід (ч)	[pi'dzɛmnij pɛrɛ'hid]
to cross (~ the street)	переходити	[pɛrɛ'hɔditi]
pedestrian	пішохід (ч)	[piʃo'hid]
sidewalk	тротуар (ч)	[trotu'ar]

bridge	міст (ч)	[mist]
embankment (river walk)	набережна (ж)	['nabɛrɛʒna]
fountain	фонтан (ч)	[fon'tan]

allée (garden walkway)	алея (ж)	[a'lɛʲa]
park	парк (ч)	[park]
boulevard	бульвар (ч)	[bulʲ'war]
square	площа (ж)	['plɔɕa]
avenue (wide street)	проспект (ч)	[pros'pɛkt]
street	вулиця (ж)	['wulitsʲa]
side street	провулок (ч)	[pro'wulok]
dead end	глухий кут (ч)	[ɦlu'hij kut]

house	будинок (ч)	[bu'dinok]
building	споруда (ж)	[spo'ruda]
skyscraper	хмарочос (ч)	[hmaro'tʃɔs]

facade	фасад (ч)	[fa'sad]
roof	дах (ч)	[dah]
window	вікно (с)	[wik'nɔ]

arch	арка (ж)	['arka]
column	колона (ж)	[ko'lɔna]
corner	ріг (ч)	[riɦ]

store window	вітрина (ж)	[wi'trina]
signboard (store sign, etc.)	вивіска (ж)	['wiwiska]
poster	афіша (ж)	[a'fiʃa]
advertising poster	рекламний плакат (ч)	[rɛk'lamnij pla'kat]
billboard	рекламний щит (ч)	[rɛk'lamnij ɕit]

garbage, trash	сміття (с)	[smit't'a]
trashcan (public ~)	урна (ж)	['urna]
to litter (vi)	смітити	[smi'titi]
garbage dump	смітник (ч)	[smit'nik]

phone booth	телефонна будка (ж)	[tɛlɛ'fɔna 'budka]
lamppost	ліхтарний стовп (ч)	[lih'tarnij stowp]
bench (park ~)	лавка (ж)	['lawka]

police officer	поліцейський (ч)	[poli'tsɛjsʲkij]
police	поліція (ж)	[po'litsiʲa]
beggar	жебрак (ч)	[ʒɛb'rak]
homeless (n)	безпритульний (ч)	[bɛzpri'tulʲnij]

29. Urban institutions

store	магазин (ч)	[maɦa'zin]
drugstore, pharmacy	аптека (ж)	[ap'tɛka]
eyeglass store	оптика (ж)	['ɔptika]
shopping mall	торгівельний центр (ч)	[torɦi'wɛlʲnij 'tsɛntr]
supermarket	супермаркет (ч)	[supɛr'markɛt]

bakery	булочна (ж)	['bulotʃna]
baker	пекар (ч)	['pɛkar]
pastry shop	кондитерська (ж)	[kon'ditɛrsʲka]
grocery store	бакалія (ж)	[baka'liʲa]
butcher shop	м'ясний магазин (ч)	[mʲas'nij maɦa'zin]

| produce store | овочевий магазин (ч) | [owo'tʃɛwij maɦa'zin] |
| market | ринок (ч) | ['rinok] |

coffee house	кав'ярня (ж)	[ka'wʲarnʲa]
restaurant	ресторан (ч)	[rɛsto'ran]
pub, bar	пивна (ж)	[piw'na]
pizzeria	піцерія (ж)	[pitsɛ'riʲa]

hair salon	перукарня (ж)	[pɛru'karnʲa]
post office	пошта (ж)	['pɔʃta]
dry cleaners	хімчистка (ж)	[him'tʃistka]
photo studio	фотоательє (с)	[fotoatɛ'ljɛ]

shoe store	взуттєвий магазин (ч)	[wzut'tɛwij maɦa'zin]
bookstore	книгарня (ж)	[kni'ɦarnʲa]
sporting goods store	спортивний магазин (ч)	[spor'tiwnij maɦa'zin]

clothes repair shop	ремонт (ч) одягу	[rɛ'mɔnt 'ɔdʲaɦu]
formal wear rental	прокат (ч) одягу	[pro'kat 'ɔdʲaɦu]
video rental store	прокат (ч) фільмів	[pro'kat 'filʲmiw]

circus	цирк (ч)	[tsirk]
zoo	зоопарк (ч)	[zoo'park]
movie theater	кінотеатр (ч)	[kinotɛ'atr]
museum	музей (ч)	[mu'zɛj]
library	бібліотека (ж)	[biblio'tɛka]

theater	театр (ч)	[tɛ'atr]
opera (opera house)	опера (ж)	['ɔpɛra]
nightclub	нічний клуб (ч)	[nitʃ'nij klub]
casino	казино (с)	[kazi'nɔ]

mosque	мечеть (ж)	[mɛ'tʃɛtʲ]
synagogue	синагога (ж)	[sina'ɦɔɦa]
cathedral	собор (ч)	[so'bɔr]
temple	храм (ч)	[hram]
church	церква (ж)	['tsɛrkwa]

college	інститут (ч)	[insti'tut]
university	університет (ч)	[uniwɛrsi'tɛt]
school	школа (ж)	['ʃkɔla]

prefecture	префектура (ж)	[prɛfɛk'tura]
city hall	мерія (ж)	['mɛriʲa]
hotel	готель (ч)	[ɦo'tɛlʲ]
bank	банк (ч)	[bank]

embassy	посольство (с)	[po'sɔlʲstwo]
travel agency	турагентство (с)	[tura'ɦɛntstwo]
information office	довідкове бюро (с)	[dowid'kɔwɛ bʲu'rɔ]
currency exchange	обмінний пункт (ч)	[ob'minij punkt]

subway	метро (с)	[mɛt'rɔ]
hospital	лікарня (ж)	[li'karnʲa]

gas station	бензоколонка (ж)	[bɛnzoko'lɔnka]
parking lot	стоянка (ж)	[sto'ʲanka]

30. Signs

signboard (store sign, etc.)	вивіска (ж)	['wiwiska]
notice (door sign, etc.)	напис (ч)	['napis]
poster	плакат (ч)	[pla'kat]

| direction sign | дороговказ (ч) | [doroɦow'kaz] |
| arrow (sign) | стрілка (ж) | ['strilka] |

caution	застереження (с)	[zastɛ'rɛʒɛnʲa]
warning sign	попередження (с)	[popɛ'rɛdʒɛnʲa]
to warn (vt)	попереджувати	[popɛ'rɛdʒuwati]

rest day (weekly ~)	вихідний день (ч)	[wiɦid'nij dɛnʲ]
timetable (schedule)	розклад (ч)	['rɔzklad]
opening hours	години (мн) роботи	[ɦo'dini ro'bɔti]

WELCOME!	ЛАСКАВО ПРОСИМО!	[las'kawo 'prɔsimo]
ENTRANCE	ВХІД	[whid]
EXIT	ВИХІД	['wiɦid]

PUSH	ВІД СЕБЕ	[wid 'sɛbɛ]
PULL	ДО СЕБЕ	[do 'sɛbɛ]
OPEN	ВІДЧИНЕНО	[wid'ʧinɛno]
CLOSED	ЗАЧИНЕНО	[za'ʧinɛno]

| WOMEN | ДЛЯ ЖІНОК | [dlʲa ʒi'nɔk] |
| MEN | ДЛЯ ЧОЛОВІКІВ | [dlʲa ʧolowi'kiw] |

DISCOUNTS	ЗНИЖКИ	['zniʒki]
SALE	РОЗПРОДАЖ	[rozp'rɔdaʒ]
NEW!	НОВИНКА!	[no'winka]
FREE	БЕЗКОШТОВНО	[bɛzkoʃ'tɔwno]

ATTENTION!	УВАГА!	[u'waɦa]
NO VACANCIES	МІСЦЬ НЕМАЄ	[misʦ nɛ'maɛ]
RESERVED	ЗАРЕЗЕРВОВАНО	[zarɛzɛr'wowano]

| ADMINISTRATION | АДМІНІСТРАЦІЯ | [admini'straʦiʲa] |
| STAFF ONLY | ТІЛЬКИ ДЛЯ ПЕРСОНАЛУ | ['tilʲki dlʲa pɛrso'nalu] |

BEWARE OF THE DOG!	ОБЕРЕЖНО! ЗЛИЙ ПЕС	[obɛ'rɛʒno! zlij pɛs]
NO SMOKING	ПАЛИТИ ЗАБОРОНЕНО	[pa'liti zabo'rɔnɛno]
DO NOT TOUCH!	НЕ ТОРКАТИСЯ!	[nɛ tor'katisʲa]

DANGEROUS	НЕБЕЗПЕЧНО	[nɛbɛz'pɛʧno]
DANGER	НЕБЕЗПЕКА	[nɛbɛz'pɛka]
HIGH VOLTAGE	ВИСОКА НАПРУГА	[wi'sɔka na'pruɦa]

| NO SWIMMING! | КУПАТИСЯ ЗАБОРОНЕНО | [ku'patisʲa zabo'rɔnɛno] |

| OUT OF ORDER | НЕ ПРАЦЮЄ | [nɛ pra'ʦʲuɛ] |

FLAMMABLE	ВОГНЕНЕБЕЗПЕЧНО	[woɦnɛnɛbɛz'pɛʧno]
FORBIDDEN	ЗАБОРОНЕНО	[zabo'rɔnɛno]
NO TRESPASSING!	ПРОХІД ЗАБОРОНЕНО	[pro'hid zabo'rɔnɛno]
WET PAINT	ПОФАРБОВАНО	[pofar'bɔwano]

31. Shopping

to buy (purchase)	купляти	[kup'lʲati]
purchase	покупка (ж)	[po'kupka]
to go shopping	робити покупки	[ro'biti po'kupki]
shopping	шопінг (ч)	['ʃopinɦ]

| to be open (ab. store) | працювати | [pratsʲu'wati] |
| to be closed | зачинитися | [zatʃi'nitisʲa] |

footwear, shoes	взуття (с)	[wzut'tʲa]
clothes, clothing	одяг (ч)	['ɔdʲaɦ]
cosmetics	косметика (ж)	[kos'mɛtika]
food products	продукти (мн)	[pro'dukti]
gift, present	подарунок (ч)	[poda'runok]

| salesman | продавець (ч) | [proda'wɛts] |
| saleswoman | продавщиця (ж) | [prodaw'ɕitsʲa] |

check out, cash desk	каса (ж)	['kasa]
mirror	дзеркало (с)	['dzɛrkalo]
counter (store ~)	прилавок (ч)	[pri'lawok]
fitting room	примірочна (ж)	[pri'mirotʃna]

to try on	приміряти	[pri'mirʲati]
to fit (ab. dress, etc.)	пасувати	[pasu'wati]
to like (I like …)	подобатися	[po'dɔbatisʲa]

price	ціна (ж)	[tsi'na]
price tag	цінник (ч)	['tsinik]
to cost (vt)	коштувати	['kɔʃtuwati]
How much?	Скільки?	['skilʲki]
discount	знижка (ж)	['zniʒka]

inexpensive (adj)	недорогий	[nɛdoro'ɦij]
cheap (adj)	дешевий	[dɛ'ʃewij]
expensive (adj)	дорогий	[doro'ɦij]
It's expensive	Це дорого.	[tsɛ 'dɔroɦo]

rental (n)	прокат (ч)	[pro'kat]
to rent (~ a tuxedo)	взяти напрокат	['wzʲati napro'kat]
credit (trade credit)	кредит (ч)	[krɛ'dit]
on credit (adv)	в кредит (ч)	[w krɛ'dit]

CLOTHING & ACCESSORIES

T&P Books Publishing

32. Outerwear. Coats

clothes	одяг (ч)	['ɔdʲaɦ]
outerwear	верхній одяг (ч)	['wɛrhnij 'ɔdʲaɦ]
winter clothing	зимовий одяг (ч)	[zɨ'mɔwɨj 'ɔdʲaɦ]
coat (overcoat)	пальто (с)	[palʲ'tɔ]
fur coat	шуба (ж)	['ʃuba]
fur jacket	кожушок (ч)	[koʒu'ʃɔk]
down coat	пуховик (ч)	[puho'wɨk]
jacket (e.g., leather ~)	куртка (ж)	['kurtka]
raincoat (trenchcoat, etc.)	плащ (ч)	[plaɕ]
waterproof (adj)	непромокальний	[nɛpromo'kalʲnɨj]

33. Men's & women's clothing

shirt (button shirt)	сорочка (ж)	[so'rɔtʃka]
pants	штани (мн)	[ʃta'nɨ]
jeans	джинси (мн)	['dʒɨnsɨ]
suit jacket	піджак (ч)	[pi'dʒak]
suit	костюм (ч)	[kos'tʲum]
dress (frock)	сукня (ж)	['suknʲa]
skirt	спідниця (ж)	[spid'nɨtsʲa]
blouse	блузка (ж)	['bluzka]
knitted jacket (cardigan, etc.)	кофта (ж)	['kɔfta]
jacket (of woman's suit)	жакет (ч)	[ʒa'kɛt]
T-shirt	футболка (ж)	[fut'bɔlka]
shorts (short trousers)	шорти (мн)	['ʃɔrtɨ]
tracksuit	спортивний костюм (ч)	[spor'tɨwnɨj kos'tʲum]
bathrobe	халат (ч)	[ha'lat]
pajamas	піжама (ж)	[pi'ʒama]
sweater	светр (ч)	[swɛtr]
pullover	пуловер (ч)	[pulo'wɛr]
vest	жилет (ч)	[ʒi'lɛt]
tailcoat	фрак (ч)	[frak]
tuxedo	смокінг (ч)	['smɔkinɦ]
uniform	форма (ж)	['fɔrma]
workwear	робочий одяг (ж)	[ro'bɔtʃij 'ɔdʲaɦ]

| overalls | комбінезон (ч) | [kombinɛ'zɔn] |
| coat (e.g., doctor's smock) | халат (ч) | [ha'lat] |

34. Clothing. Underwear

underwear	білизна (ж)	[bi'lizna]
undershirt (A-shirt)	майка (ж)	['majka]
socks	шкарпетки (мн)	[ʃkar'pɛtki]

nightgown	нічна сорочка (ж)	[nitʃ'na so'rɔtʃka]
bra	бюстгальтер (ч)	[bʲustʲhalʲtɛr]
knee highs	гольфи (мн)	['hɔlʲfi]
(knee-high socks)		

pantyhose	колготки (мн)	[kol'hɔtki]
stockings (thigh highs)	панчохи (мн)	[pan'tʃɔhi]
bathing suit	купальник (ч)	[ku'palʲnik]

35. Headwear

hat	шапка (ж)	['ʃapka]
fedora	капелюх (ч)	[kapɛ'lʲuh]
baseball cap	бейсболка (ж)	[bɛjs'bɔlka]
flatcap	кашкет (ч)	[kaʃ'kɛt]

beret	берет (ч)	[bɛ'rɛt]
hood	каптур (ч)	[kap'tur]
panama hat	панамка (ж)	[pa'namka]
knit cap (knitted hat)	в'язана шапочка (ж)	['wʲazana 'ʃapotʃka]

| headscarf | хустка (ж) | ['hustka] |
| women's hat | капелюшок (ч) | [kapɛ'lʲuʃok] |

hard hat	каска (ж)	['kaska]
garrison cap	пілотка (ж)	[pi'lɔtka]
helmet	шолом (ч)	[ʃo'lɔm]

| derby | котелок (ч) | [kotɛ'lɔk] |
| top hat | циліндр (ч) | [tsi'lindr] |

36. Footwear

footwear	взуття (с)	[wzut'tʲa]
shoes (men's shoes)	черевики (мн)	[tʃɛrɛ'wiki]
shoes (women's shoes)	туфлі (мн)	['tufli]
boots (e.g., cowboy ~)	чоботи (мн)	['tʃɔboti]
slippers	капці (мн)	['kaptsi]

tennis shoes (e.g., Nike ~)	кросівки (мн)	[kro'siwki]
sneakers (e.g., Converse ~)	кеди (мн)	['kɛdi]
sandals	сандалі (мн)	[san'dali]

cobbler (shoe repairer)	чоботар (ч)	[tʃobo'tar]
heel	каблук (ч)	[kab'luk]
pair (of shoes)	пара (ж)	['para]

shoestring	шнурок (ч)	[ʃnu'rɔk]
to lace (vt)	шнурувати	[ʃnuru'wati]
shoehorn	ложка (ж)	['lɔʒka]
shoe polish	крем (ч) для взуття	[krɛm dlʲa wzut'tʲa]

37. Personal accessories

gloves	рукавички (мн)	[ruka'witʃki]
mittens	рукавиці (мн)	[ruka'witsi]
scarf (muffler)	шарф (ч)	[ʃarf]

glasses (eyeglasses)	окуляри (мн)	[oku'lʲari]
frame (eyeglass ~)	оправа (ж)	[op'rawa]
umbrella	парасолька (ж)	[para'sɔlʲka]
walking stick	ціпок (ч)	[tsi'pɔk]
hairbrush	щітка (ж) для волосся	['ɕitka dlʲa wo'lɔssʲa]
fan	віяло (с)	['wiʲalo]

tie (necktie)	краватка (ж)	[kra'watka]
bow tie	краватка-метелик (ж)	[kra'watka mɛ'tɛlik]
suspenders	шлейки (мн)	['ʃlɛjki]
handkerchief	носовичок (ч)	[nosowi'tʃɔk]

comb	гребінець (ч)	[ɦrɛbi'nɛts]
barrette	заколка (ж)	[za'kɔlka]
hairpin	шпилька (ж)	['ʃpilʲka]
buckle	пряжка (ж)	['prʲaʒka]

| belt | пасок (ч) | ['pasok] |
| shoulder strap | ремінь (ч) | ['rɛminʲ] |

bag (handbag)	сумка (ж)	['sumka]
purse	сумочка (ж)	['sumotʃka]
backpack	рюкзак (ч)	[rʲuk'zak]

38. Clothing. Miscellaneous

| fashion | мода (ж) | ['mɔda] |
| in vogue (adj) | модний | ['mɔdnij] |

fashion designer	модельєр (ч)	[modɛ'ljɛr]
collar	комір (ч)	['kɔmir]
pocket	кишеня (ж)	[ki'ʃɛnʲa]
pocket (as adj)	кишеньковий	[kiʃɛnʲ'kɔwij]
sleeve	рукав (ч)	[ru'kaw]
hanging loop	петелька (ж)	[pɛ'tɛlʲka]
fly (on trousers)	ширінка (ж)	[ʃi'rinka]

zipper (fastener)	змійка (ж)	['zmijka]
fastener	застібка (ж)	['zastibka]
button	ґудзик (ч)	['gudzik]
buttonhole	петля (ж)	[pɛt'lʲa]
to come off (ab. button)	відірватися	[widir'watisʲa]

to sew (vi, vt)	шити	['ʃiti]
to embroider (vi, vt)	вишивати	[wiʃi'wati]
embroidery	вишивка (ж)	['wiʃiwka]
sewing needle	голка (ж)	['hɔlka]
thread	нитка (ж)	['nitka]
seam	шов (ч)	[ʃow]

to get dirty (vi)	забруднитися	[zabrud'nitisʲa]
stain (mark, spot)	пляма (ж)	['plʲama]
to crease, crumple (vi)	пом'ятися	[po'mʲ/atisʲa]
to tear, to rip (vt)	порвати	[por'wati]
clothes moth	міль (ж)	[milʲ]

39. Personal care. Cosmetics

toothpaste	зубна паста (ж)	[zub'na 'pasta]
toothbrush	зубна щітка (ж)	[zub'na 'ɕitka]
to brush one's teeth	чистити зуби	['tʃistiti 'zubi]

razor	бритва (ж)	['britwa]
shaving cream	крем (ч) для гоління	[krɛm dlʲa ɦo'linʲa]
to shave (vi)	голитися	[ɦo'litisʲa]

| soap | мило (с) | ['miɫo] |
| shampoo | шампунь (ч) | [ʃam'punʲ] |

scissors	ножиці (мн)	['nɔʒitsi]
nail file	пилочка (ж) для нігтів	['piɫotʃka dlʲa 'niɦtiw]
nail clippers	щипчики (мн)	['ɕiptʃiki]
tweezers	пінцет (ч)	[pin'tsɛt]

cosmetics	косметика (ж)	[kos'mɛtika]
face mask	маска (ж)	['maska]
manicure	манікюр (ч)	[mani'kʲur]
to have a manicure	робити манікюр	[ro'biti mani'kʲur]
pedicure	педикюр (ч)	[pɛdi'kʲur]

make-up bag	косметичка (ж)	[kosmɛ'titʃka]
face powder	пудра (ж)	['pudra]
powder compact	пудрениця (ж)	['pudrɛnitsʲa]
blusher	рум'яна (мн)	[ru'mʲana]

perfume (bottled)	парфуми (мн)	[par'fumɨ]
toilet water (lotion)	туалетна вода (ж)	[tua'lɛtna wo'da]
lotion	лосьйон (ч)	[lo'sjon]
cologne	одеколон (ч)	[odɛko'lon]

eyeshadow	тіні (мн) для повік	['tini dlʲa po'wik]
eyeliner	олівець (ч) для очей	[oli'wɛts dlʲa o'tʃɛj]
mascara	туш (ж)	[tuʃ]

lipstick	губна помада (ж)	[hub'na po'mada]
nail polish, enamel	лак (ч) для нігтів	[lak dlʲa 'nihtiw]
hair spray	лак (ч) для волосся	[lak dlʲa wo'lɔssʲa]
deodorant	дезодорант (ч)	[dɛzodo'rant]

cream	крем (ч)	[krɛm]
face cream	крем (ч) для обличчя	[krɛm dlʲa ob'litʃʲa]
hand cream	крем (ч) для рук	[krɛm dlʲa ruk]
anti-wrinkle cream	крем (ч) проти зморшок	[krɛm 'prɔtɨ 'zmɔrʃok]
day (as adj)	денний	['dɛnij]
night (as adj)	нічний	[nitʃ'nij]

tampon	тампон (ч)	[tam'pɔn]
toilet paper (toilet roll)	туалетний папір (ч)	[tua'lɛtnij pa'pir]
hair dryer	фен (ч)	[fɛn]

40. Watches. Clocks

watch (wristwatch)	годинник (ч)	[ɦo'dinik]
dial	циферблат (ч)	[tsifɛrb'lat]
hand (of clock, watch)	стрілка (ж)	['strilka]
metal watch band	браслет (ч)	[bras'lɛt]
watch strap	ремінець (ч)	[rɛmi'nɛts]

battery	батарейка (ж)	[bata'rɛjka]
to be dead (battery)	сісти	['sisti]
to change a battery	поміняти батарейку	[pomi'nʲati bata'rɛjku]
to run fast	поспішати	[pospi'ʃati]
to run slow	відставати	[widsta'wati]

wall clock	годинник (ч)	[ɦo'dinik]
hourglass	годинник (ч) пісковий	[ɦo'dinik pis'kɔwij]
sundial	годинник (ч) сонячний	[ɦo'dinik 'sɔnʲatʃnij]
alarm clock	будильник (ч)	[bu'dilʲnik]
watchmaker	годинникар (ч)	[ɦodini'kar]
to repair (vt)	ремонтувати	[rɛmontu'wati]

EVERYDAY EXPERIENCE

T&P Books Publishing

41. Money

money	гроші (мн)	['ɦrɔʃi]
currency exchange	обмін (ч)	['ɔbmin]
exchange rate	курс (ч)	[kurs]
ATM	банкомат (ч)	[banko'mat]
coin	монета (ж)	[mo'nɛta]
dollar	долар (ч)	['dɔlar]
euro	євро (ч)	['ɛwro]
lira	ліра (ж)	['lira]
Deutschmark	марка (ж)	['marka]
franc	франк (ч)	['frank]
pound sterling	фунт (ч)	['funt]
yen	ієна (ж)	[i'ɛna]
debt	борг (ч)	['bɔrɦ]
debtor	боржник (ч)	[borʒ'nik]
to lend (money)	позичити	[po'zitʃiti]
to borrow (vi, vt)	взяти в борг	['wzʲati w borɦ]
bank	банк (ч)	[bank]
account	рахунок (ч)	[ra'hunok]
to deposit into the account	покласти на рахунок	[pok'lasti na ra'hunok]
to withdraw (vt)	зняти з рахунку	['znʲati z ra'hunku]
credit card	кредитна картка (ж)	[krɛ'ditna 'kartka]
cash	готівка (ж)	[ɦo'tiwka]
check	чек (ч)	[tʃɛk]
to write a check	виписати чек	['wipisati 'tʃɛk]
checkbook	чекова книжка (ж)	['tʃɛkowa 'kniʒka]
wallet	гаманець (ч)	[ɦama'nɛts]
change purse	гаманець (ч)	[ɦama'nɛts]
safe	сейф (ч)	[sɛjf]
heir	спадкоємець (ч)	[spadko'ɛmɛts]
inheritance	спадщина (с)	['spadɕina]
fortune (wealth)	статок (ч)	['statok]
lease	оренда (ж)	[o'rɛnda]
rent (money)	квартирна плата (ж)	[kwar'tirna 'plata]
to rent (sth from sb)	наймати	[naj'mati]
price	ціна (ж)	[tsi'na]
cost	вартість (ж)	['wartistʲ]

sum	сума (ж)	['suma]
to spend (vt)	витрачати	[witra'tʃati]
expenses	витрати (мн)	['witrati]
to economize (vi, vt)	економити	[ɛko'nɔmiti]
economical	економний	[ɛko'nɔmnij]
to pay (vi, vt)	платити	[pla'titi]
payment	оплата (ж)	[op'lata]
change (give the ~)	решта (ж)	['rɛʃta]
tax	податок (ч)	[po'datok]
fine	штраф (ч)	[ʃtraf]
to fine (vt)	штрафувати	[ʃtrafu'wati]

42. Post. Postal service

post office	пошта (ж)	['pɔʃta]
mail (letters, etc.)	пошта (ж)	['pɔʃta]
mailman	листоноша (ч)	[listo'nɔʃa]
opening hours	години (мн) роботи	[ɦo'dini ro'bɔti]
letter	лист (ч)	[list]
registered letter	рекомендований лист (ч)	[rɛkomɛn'dɔwanij list]
postcard	листівка (ж)	[lis'tiwka]
telegram	телеграма (ж)	[tɛlɛ'ɦrama]
package (parcel)	посилка (ж)	[po'silka]
money transfer	грошовий переказ (ч)	[ɦroʃo'wij pɛ'rɛkaz]
to receive (vt)	отримати	[ot'rimati]
to send (vt)	відправити	[wid'prawiti]
sending	відправлення (с)	[wid'prawlɛnʲa]
address	адреса (ж)	[ad'rɛsa]
ZIP code	індекс (ч)	['indɛks]
sender	відправник (ч)	[wid'prawnik]
receiver	одержувач (ч)	[o'dɛrʒuwatʃ]
name (first name)	ім'я (с)	[i'mʲia]
surname (last name)	прізвище (с)	['prizwiɕɛ]
postage rate	тариф (ч)	[ta'rif]
standard (adj)	звичайний	[zwi'tʃajnij]
economical (adj)	економічний	[ɛkono'mitʃnij]
weight	вага (ж)	[wa'ɦa]
to weigh (~ letters)	важити	['waʒiti]
envelope	конверт (ч)	[kon'wɛrt]
postage stamp	марка (ж)	['marka]

43. Banking

bank	банк (ч)	[bank]
branch (of bank, etc.)	відділення (с)	[wid'dilɛnʲa]
bank clerk, consultant	консультант (ч)	[konsulʲ'tant]
manager (director)	управляючий (ч)	[upraw'lʲaʲutʃij]
bank account	рахунок (ч)	[ra'hunok]
account number	номер (ч) рахунка	['nɔmɛr ra'hunka]
checking account	поточний рахунок (ч)	[po'tɔtʃnij ra'hunok]
savings account	накопичувальний рахунок (ч)	[nako'pitʃuwalʲnij ra'hunok]
to open an account	відкрити рахунок	[wid'kriti ra'hunok]
to close the account	закрити рахунок	[za'kriti ra'hunok]
to deposit into the account	покласти на рахунок	[pok'lasti na ra'hunok]
to withdraw (vt)	зняти з рахунку	['znʲati z ra'hunku]
deposit	внесок (ч)	['wnɛsok]
to make a deposit	зробити внесок	[zro'biti 'wnɛsok]
wire transfer	переказ (ч)	[pɛ'rɛkaz]
to wire, to transfer	зробити переказ	[zro'biti pɛ'rɛkaz]
sum	сума (ж)	['suma]
How much?	Скільки?	['skilʲki]
signature	підпис (ч)	['pidpis]
to sign (vt)	підписати	[pidpɪ'sati]
credit card	кредитна картка (ж)	[krɛ'ditna 'kartka]
code (PIN code)	код (ч)	[kod]
credit card number	номер (ч) кредитної картки	['nɔmɛr krɛ'ditnoji 'kartki]
ATM	банкомат (ч)	[banko'mat]
check	чек (ч)	[tʃɛk]
to write a check	виписати чек	['wipisati 'tʃɛk]
checkbook	чекова книжка (ж)	['tʃɛkowa 'kniʒka]
loan (bank ~)	кредит (ч)	[krɛ'dit]
to apply for a loan	звертатися за кредитом	[zwɛr'tatisʲa za krɛ'ditom]
to get a loan	брати кредит	['brati krɛ'dit]
to give a loan	надавати кредит	[nada'wati krɛ'dit]
guarantee	застава (ж)	[za'stawa]

44. Telephone. Phone conversation

| telephone | телефон (ч) | [tɛlɛ'fɔn] |
| cell phone | мобільний телефон (ч) | [mo'bilʲnij tɛlɛ'fɔn] |

answering machine	автовідповідач (ч)	[awtowidpowi'datʃ]
to call (by phone)	телефонувати	[tɛlɛfonu'wati]
phone call	дзвінок (ч)	[dzwi'nɔk]

to dial a number	набрати номер	[nab'rati 'nɔmɛr]
Hello!	Алло!	[a'lɔ]
to ask (vt)	запитати	[zapi'tati]
to answer (vi, vt)	відповісти	[widpo'wisti]

to hear (vt)	чути	['tʃuti]
well (adv)	добре	['dɔbrɛ]
not well (adv)	погано	[po'ɦano]
noises (interference)	перешкоди (мн)	[pɛrɛʃ'kɔdi]

receiver	трубка (ж)	['trubka]
to pick up (~ the phone)	зняти трубку	['znʲati 'trubku]
to hang up (~ the phone)	покласти трубку	[pok'lasti t'rubku]

busy (engaged)	зайнятий	['zajnʲatij]
to ring (ab. phone)	дзвонити	[dzwo'niti]
telephone book	телефонна книга (ж)	[tɛlɛ'fɔna 'kniɦa]

local (adj)	місцевий	[mis'tsɛwij]
local call	місцевий зв'язок (ч)	[mis'tsɛwij 'zwʲazok]
long distance (~ call)	міжміський	[miʒmis'ʲkij]
long-distance call	міжміський зв'язок (ч)	[miʒmis'ʲkij 'zwʲazok]
international (adj)	міжнародний	[miʒna'rɔdnij]
international call	міжнародний зв'язок (ч)	[miʒna'rɔdnij 'zwʲazok]

45. Cell phone

cell phone	мобільний телефон (ч)	[mo'bilʲnij tɛlɛ'fɔn]
display	дисплей (ч)	[dis'plɛj]
button	кнопка (ж)	['knɔpka]
SIM card	SIM-карта (ж)	[sim 'karta]

battery	батарея (ж)	[bata'rɛʲa]
to be dead (battery)	розрядитися	[rozrʲa'ditisʲa]
charger	зарядний пристрій (ч)	[za'rʲadnij 'pristrij]
menu	меню (с)	[mɛ'nʲu]
settings	настройки (мн)	[na'strɔjki]
tune (melody)	мелодія (ж)	[mɛ'lɔdiʲa]
to select (vt)	вибрати	['wibrati]

calculator	калькулятор (ч)	[kalʲku'lʲator]
voice mail	автовідповідач (ч)	[awtowidpowi'datʃ]
alarm clock	будильник (ч)	[bu'dilʲnik]
contacts	телефонна книга (ж)	[tɛlɛ'fɔna 'kniɦa]
SMS (text message)	SMS-повідомлення (с)	[ɛsɛ'mɛs powi'dɔmlɛnʲa]
subscriber	абонент (ч)	[abo'nɛnt]

46. Stationery

| ballpoint pen | авторучка (ж) | [awto'rutʃka] |
| fountain pen | ручка-перо (c) | ['rutʃka pɛ'rɔ] |

pencil	олівець (ч)	[oli'wɛts]
highlighter	маркер (ч)	['markɛr]
felt-tip pen	фломастер (ч)	[flo'mastɛr]

| notepad | блокнот (ч) | [blok'nɔt] |
| agenda (diary) | щоденник (ч) | [ɕo'dɛnik] |

ruler	лінійка (ж)	[li'nijka]
calculator	калькулятор (ч)	[kalʲku'lʲator]
eraser	гумка (ж)	['ɦumka]
thumbtack	кнопка (ж)	['knɔpka]
paper clip	скріпка (ж)	['skripka]

glue	клей (ч)	[klɛj]
stapler	степлер (ч)	['stɛplɛr]
hole punch	діркопробивач (ч)	[dirkoprobi'watʃ]
pencil sharpener	стругачка (ж)	[stru'ɦatʃka]

47. Foreign languages

language	мова (ж)	['mɔwa]
foreign language	іноземна мова (ж)	[ino'zɛmna 'mɔwa]
to study (vt)	вивчати	[wiw'tʃati]
to learn (language, etc.)	вчити	['wtʃiti]

to read (vi, vt)	читати	[tʃi'tati]
to speak (vi, vt)	розмовляти	[rozmow'lʲati]
to understand (vt)	розуміти	[rozu'miti]
to write (vt)	писати	[pi'sati]

fast (adv)	швидко	['ʃwidko]
slowly (adv)	повільно	[po'wilʲno]
fluently (adv)	вільно	['wilʲno]

rules	правила (мн)	['prawila]
grammar	граматика (ж)	[ɦra'matika]
vocabulary	лексика (ж)	['lɛksika]
phonetics	фонетика (ж)	[fo'nɛtika]

textbook	підручник (ч)	[pid'rutʃnik]
dictionary	словник (ч)	[slow'nik]
teach-yourself book	самовчитель (ч)	[samow'tʃitɛlʲ]
phrasebook	розмовник (ч)	[roz'mɔwnik]
cassette, tape	касета (ж)	[ka'sɛta]

videotape	відеокасета (ж)	['wideo ka'seta]
CD, compact disc	CD-диск (ч)	[si'di disk]
DVD	DVD (ч)	[diwi'di]

alphabet	алфавіт (ч)	[alfa'wit]
to spell (vt)	говорити по буквах	[howo'riti po 'bukwah]
pronunciation	вимова (ж)	[wi'mɔwa]

accent	акцент (ч)	[ak'tsɛnt]
with an accent	з акцентом	[z ak'tsɛntom]
without an accent	без акценту (ч)	[bɛz ak'tsɛntu]

| word | слово (с) | ['slɔwo] |
| meaning | сенс (ч) | [sɛns] |

course (e.g., a French ~)	курси (мн)	['kursi]
to sign up	записатися	[zapi'satisʲa]
teacher	викладач (ч)	[wikla'datʃ]

translation (process)	переклад (ч)	[pɛ'rɛklad]
translation (text, etc.)	переклад (ч)	[pɛ'rɛklad]
translator	перекладач (ч)	[pɛrɛkla'datʃ]
interpreter	перекладач (ч)	[pɛrɛkla'datʃ]

| polyglot | поліглот (ч) | [poliɦ'lɔt] |
| memory | пам'ять (ж) | ['pamʲatʲ] |

MEALS. RESTAURANT

T&P Books Publishing

48. Table setting

spoon	ложка (ж)	['lɔʒka]
knife	ніж (ч)	[niʒ]
fork	виделка (ж)	[wi'dɛlka]

cup (e.g., coffee ~)	чашка (ж)	['ʧaʃka]
plate (dinner ~)	тарілка (ж)	[ta'rilka]
saucer	блюдце (с)	['blʲudtsɛ]
napkin (on table)	серветка (ж)	[sɛr'wɛtka]
toothpick	зубочистка (ж)	[zubo'ʧistka]

49. Restaurant

restaurant	ресторан (ч)	[rɛsto'ran]
coffee house	кав'ярня (ж)	[ka'wʲarnʲa]
pub, bar	бар (ч)	[bar]
tearoom	чайна (ж)	['ʧajna]

waiter	офіціант (ч)	[ofitsi'ant]
waitress	офіціантка (ж)	[ofitsi'antka]
bartender	бармен (ч)	[bar'mɛn]
menu	меню (с)	[mɛ'nʲu]
wine list	карта (ж) вин	['karta win]
to book a table	забронювати столик	[zabronʲu'watɨ 'stɔlik]

course, dish	страва (ж)	['strawa]
to order (meal)	замовити	[za'mɔwiti]
to make an order	зробити замовлення	[zro'biti za'mɔwlɛnʲa]
aperitif	аперитив (ч)	[apɛrɨ'tiw]
appetizer	закуска (ж)	[za'kuska]
dessert	десерт (ч)	[dɛ'sɛrt]

check	рахунок (ч)	[ra'hunok]
to pay the check	оплатити рахунок	[opla'titi ra'hunok]
to give change	дати решту	['dati 'rɛʃtu]
tip	чайові (мн)	[ʧajʲo'wi]

50. Meals

| food | їжа (ж) | ['jіʒa] |
| to eat (vi, vt) | їсти | ['jіsti] |

breakfast	сніданок (ч)	[sni'danok]
to have breakfast	снідати	['snidati]
lunch	обід (ч)	[o'bid]
to have lunch	обідати	[o'bidati]
dinner	вечеря (ж)	[wɛ'tʃɛrʲa]
to have dinner	вечеряти	[wɛ'tʃɛrʲati]

appetite	апетит (ч)	[apɛ'tit]
Enjoy your meal!	Смачного!	[smatʃ'nɔɦo]

to open (~ a bottle)	відкривати	[widkrɨ'wati]
to spill (liquid)	пролити	[pro'litɨ]
to spill out (vi)	пролитись	[pro'litisʲ]

to boil (vi)	кипіти	[kɨ'piti]
to boil (vt)	кип'ятити	[kɨpʲa'tɨti]
boiled (~ water)	кип'ячений	[kɨpʲa'tʃɛnij]
to chill, cool down (vt)	охолодити	[oholo'ditɨ]
to chill (vi)	охолоджуватись	[oho'lɔdʒuwatisʲ]

taste, flavor	смак (ч)	[smak]
aftertaste	присмак (ч)	['prɨsmak]

to slim down (lose weight)	худнути	['hudnuti]
diet	дієта (ж)	[di'ɛta]
vitamin	вітамін (ч)	[wita'min]
calorie	калорія (ж)	[ka'lɔriʲa]
vegetarian (n)	вегетаріанець (ч)	[wɛɦɛtari'anɛts]
vegetarian (adj)	вегетаріанський	[wɛɦɛtari'ansʲkij]

fats (nutrient)	жири (мн)	[ʒɨ'ri]
proteins	білки (мн)	[bil'ki]
carbohydrates	вуглеводи (ч)	[wuɦlɛ'wɔdɨ]
slice (of lemon, ham)	скибка (ж)	['skɨbka]
piece (of cake, pie)	шматок (ч)	[ʃma'tɔk]
crumb (of bread, cake, etc.)	крихта (ж)	['krɨhta]

51. Cooked dishes

course, dish	страва (ж)	['strawa]
cuisine	кухня (ж)	['kuhnʲa]
recipe	рецепт (ч)	[rɛ'tsɛpt]
portion	порція (ж)	['pɔrtsiʲa]

salad	салат (ч)	[sa'lat]
soup	юшка (ж)	['ʲuʃka]

clear soup (broth)	бульйон (ч)	[bulʲon]
sandwich (bread)	канапка (ж)	[ka'napka]

fried eggs	яєчня (ж)	[jaˈɛʃnʲa]
hamburger (beefburger)	гамбургер (ч)	[ˈhamburɦɛr]
beefsteak	біфштекс (ч)	[bifˈʃtɛks]

side dish	гарнір (ч)	[harˈnir]
spaghetti	спагеті (мн)	[spaˈɦɛti]
mashed potatoes	картопляне пюре (с)	[kartopˈlʲanɛ pʲuˈrɛ]
pizza	піца (ж)	[ˈpitsa]
porridge (oatmeal, etc.)	каша (ж)	[ˈkaʃa]
omelet	омлет (ч)	[omˈlɛt]

boiled (e.g., ~ beef)	варений	[waˈrɛnij]
smoked (adj)	копчений	[kopˈtʃɛnij]
fried (adj)	смажений	[ˈsmaʒɛnij]
dried (adj)	сушений	[ˈsuʃɛnij]
frozen (adj)	заморожений	[zamoˈrɔʒɛnij]
pickled (adj)	маринований	[mariˈnɔwanij]

sweet (sugary)	солодкий	[soˈlɔdkij]
salty (adj)	солоний	[soˈlɔnij]
cold (adj)	холодний	[hoˈlɔdnij]
hot (adj)	гарячий	[haˈrʲatʃij]
bitter (adj)	гіркий	[hirˈkij]
tasty (adj)	смачний	[smatʃˈnij]

to cook in boiling water	варити	[waˈriti]
to cook (dinner)	готувати	[ɦotuˈwati]
to fry (vt)	смажити	[ˈsmaʒiti]
to heat up (food)	розігрівати	[roziɦriˈwati]

to salt (vt)	солити	[soˈliti]
to pepper (vt)	перчити	[pɛrˈtʃiti]
to grate (vt)	терти	[ˈtɛrti]
peel (n)	шкірка (ж)	[ˈʃkirka]
to peel (vt)	чистити	[ˈtʃistiti]

52. Food

meat	м'ясо (с)	[ˈmʲaso]
chicken	курка (ж)	[ˈkurka]
Rock Cornish hen (poussin)	курча (с)	[kurˈtʃa]
duck	качка (ж)	[ˈkatʃka]
goose	гусак (ч)	[ɦuˈsak]
game	дичина (ж)	[ditʃiˈna]
turkey	індичка (ж)	[inˈditʃka]

pork	свинина (ж)	[swiˈnina]
veal	телятина (ж)	[tɛˈlʲatina]
lamb	баранина (ж)	[baˈranina]

| beef | яловичина (ж) | [ˈialowitʃina] |
| rabbit | кріль (ч) | [krilʲ] |

| sausage (bologna, pepperoni, etc.) | ковбаса (ж) | [kowbaˈsa] |
| vienna sausage (frankfurter) | сосиска (ж) | [soˈsiska] |

bacon	бекон (ч)	[bɛˈkɔn]
ham	шинка (ж)	[ˈʃinka]
gammon	окіст (ч)	[ˈɔkist]

pâté	паштет (ч)	[paʃˈtɛt]
liver	печінка (ж)	[pɛˈtʃinka]
hamburger (ground beef)	фарш (ч)	[farʃ]
tongue	язик (ч)	[jaˈzik]

egg	яйце (с)	[jajˈtsɛ]
eggs	яйця (мн)	[ˈiajtsʲa]
egg white	білок (ч)	[biˈlɔk]
egg yolk	жовток (ч)	[ʒowˈtɔk]

fish	риба (ж)	[ˈriba]
seafood	морепродукти (мн)	[morɛproˈdukti]
caviar	ікра (ж)	[ikˈra]

crab	краб (ч)	[krab]
shrimp	креветка (ж)	[krɛˈwɛtka]
oyster	устриця (ж)	[ˈustritsʲa]
spiny lobster	лангуст (ч)	[lanˈɦust]
octopus	восьминіг (ч)	[wosʲmiˈniɦ]
squid	кальмар (ч)	[kalʲˈmar]

sturgeon	осетрина (ж)	[osɛtˈrina]
salmon	лосось (ч)	[loˈsɔsʲ]
halibut	палтус (ч)	[ˈpaltus]

cod	тріска (ж)	[trisˈka]
mackerel	скумбрія (ж)	[ˈskumbriʲa]
tuna	тунець (ч)	[tuˈnɛts]
eel	вугор (ч)	[wuˈɦɔr]

trout	форель (ж)	[foˈrɛlʲ]
sardine	сардина (ж)	[sarˈdina]
pike	щука (ж)	[ˈɕuka]
herring	оселедець (ч)	[osɛˈlɛdɛts]

bread	хліб (ч)	[hlib]
cheese	сир (ч)	[sir]
sugar	цукор (ч)	[ˈtsukor]
salt	сіль (ж)	[silʲ]
rice	рис (ч)	[ris]
pasta (macaroni)	макарони (мн)	[makaˈrɔni]

noodles	локшина (ж)	[lokʃi'na]
butter	вершкове масло (с)	[wɛrʃ'kɔwɛ 'maslo]
vegetable oil	олія (ж) рослинна	[o'liʲa ros'lina]
sunflower oil	соняшникова олія (ж)	['sɔnʲaʃnikowa o'liʲa]
margarine	маргарин (ч)	[marɦa'rin]

| olives | оливки (мн) | [o'liwki] |
| olive oil | олія (ж) оливкова | [o'liʲa o'liwkowa] |

milk	молоко (с)	[molo'kɔ]
condensed milk	згущене молоко (с)	['zɦuɕɛnɛ molo'kɔ]
yogurt	йогурт (ч)	['jɔɦurt]
sour cream	сметана (ж)	[smɛ'tana]
cream (of milk)	вершки (мн)	[wɛrʃ'ki]

| mayonnaise | майонез (ч) | [maʲo'nɛz] |
| buttercream | крем (ч) | [krɛm] |

cereal grains (wheat, etc.)	крупа (ж)	[kru'pa]
flour	борошно (с)	['bɔroʃno]
canned food	консерви (мн)	[kon'sɛrwi]

cornflakes	кукурудзяні пластівці (мн)	[kuku'rudzʲani plastiw'tsi]
honey	мед (ч)	[mɛd]
jam	джем (ч)	[dʒɛm]
chewing gum	жувальна гумка (ж)	[ʒu'walʲna 'ɦumka]

53. Drinks

water	вода (ж)	[wo'da]
drinking water	питна вода (ж)	[pit'na wo'da]
mineral water	мінеральна вода (ж)	[minɛ'ralʲna wo'da]

still (adj)	без газу	[bɛz 'ɦazu]
carbonated (adj)	газований	[ɦa'zowanij]
sparkling (adj)	з газом	[z 'ɦazom]
ice	лід (ч)	[lid]
with ice	з льодом	[z lʲodom]

| non-alcoholic (adj) | безалкогольний | [bɛzalko'ɦɔlʲnij] |
| soft drink | безалкогольний напій (ч) | [bɛzalko'ɦɔlʲnij na'pij] |

| refreshing drink | прохолодній напій (ч) | [proɦo'lɔdnij na'pij] |
| lemonade | лимонад (ч) | [limo'nad] |

liquors	алкогольні напої (мн)	[alko'ɦɔlʲni na'pɔji]
wine	вино (с)	[wi'nɔ]
white wine	біле вино (с)	['bilɛ wi'nɔ]
red wine	червоне вино (с)	[tʃɛr'wɔnɛ wi'nɔ]

liqueur	лікер (ч)	[li'kɛr]
champagne	шампанське (с)	[ʃam'pansʲkɛ]
vermouth	вермут (ч)	['wɛrmut]

whiskey	віскі (с)	['wiski]
vodka	горілка (ж)	[ɦo'rilka]
gin	джин (ч)	[dʒin]
cognac	коньяк (ч)	[ko'nʲak]
rum	ром (ч)	[rom]

coffee	кава (ж)	['kawa]
black coffee	чорна кава (ж)	['tʃɔrna 'kawa]
coffee with milk	кава (ж) з молоком	['kawa z molo'kɔm]
cappuccino	кава (ж) з вершками	['kawa z wɛrʃ'kamɨ]
instant coffee	розчинна кава (ж)	[roz'tʃɨna 'kawa]

milk	молоко (с)	[molo'kɔ]
cocktail	коктейль (ч)	[kok'tɛjlʲ]
milkshake	молочний коктейль (ч)	[mo'lɔtʃnij kok'tɛjlʲ]

juice	сік (ч)	[sik]
tomato juice	томатний сік (ч)	[to'matnij 'sik]
orange juice	апельсиновий сік (ч)	[apɛlʲ'sinowij sik]
freshly squeezed juice	свіжовижатий сік (ч)	[swiʒo'wiʒatij sik]

beer	пиво (с)	['pɨwo]
light beer	світле пиво (с)	['switlɛ 'pɨwo]
dark beer	темне пиво (с)	['tɛmnɛ 'pɨwo]

tea	чай (ч)	[tʃaj]
black tea	чорний чай (ч)	['tʃɔrnij tʃaj]
green tea	зелений чай (ч)	[zɛ'lɛnij tʃaj]

54. Vegetables

| vegetables | овочі (мн) | ['ɔwotʃi] |
| greens | зелень (ж) | ['zɛlɛnʲ] |

tomato	помідор (ч)	[pomi'dɔr]
cucumber	огірок (ч)	[oɦi'rɔk]
carrot	морква (ж)	['mɔrkwa]
potato	картопля (ж)	[kar'tɔplʲa]
onion	цибуля (ж)	[tsi'bulʲa]
garlic	часник (ч)	[tʃas'nik]

cabbage	капуста (ж)	[ka'pusta]
cauliflower	кольорова капуста (ж)	[kolʲo'rɔwa ka'pusta]
Brussels sprouts	брюссельська капуста (ж)	[brʲu'sɛlʲsʲka ka'pusta]
broccoli	капуста броколі (ж)	[ka'pusta 'brɔkoli]

beetroot	буряк (ч)	[bu'rʲak]
eggplant	баклажан (ч)	[bakla'ʒan]
zucchini	кабачок (ч)	[kaba'tʃɔk]
pumpkin	гарбуз (ч)	[ɦar'buz]
turnip	ріпа (ж)	['ripa]

parsley	петрушка (ж)	[pɛt'ruʃka]
dill	кріп (ч)	[krip]
lettuce	салат (ч)	[sa'lat]
celery	селера (ж)	[sɛ'lɛra]
asparagus	спаржа (ж)	['sparʒa]
spinach	шпинат (ч)	[ʃpi'nat]

pea	горох (ч)	[ɦo'rɔh]
beans	боби (мн)	[bo'bʲi]
corn (maize)	кукурудза (ж)	[kuku'rudza]
kidney bean	квасоля (ж)	[kwa'sɔlʲa]

bell pepper	перець (ч)	['pɛrɛts]
radish	редька (ж)	['rɛdʲka]
artichoke	артишок (ч)	[artiʲʃɔk]

55. Fruits. Nuts

fruit	фрукт (ч)	[frukt]
apple	яблуко (с)	['ʲabluko]
pear	груша (ж)	['ɦruʃa]
lemon	лимон (ч)	[lɨ'mɔn]
orange	апельсин (ч)	[apɛlʲ'sin]
strawberry (garden ~)	полуниця (ж)	[polu'nitsʲa]

mandarin	мандарин (ч)	[manda'rin]
plum	слива (ж)	['slɨwa]
peach	персик (ч)	['pɛrsɨk]
apricot	абрикос (ч)	[abri'kɔs]
raspberry	малина (ж)	[ma'lɨna]
pineapple	ананас (ч)	[ana'nas]

banana	банан (ч)	[ba'nan]
watermelon	кавун (ч)	[ka'wun]
grape	виноград (ч)	[wino'ɦrad]
sour cherry	вишня (ж)	['wiʃnʲa]
sweet cherry	черешня (ж)	[tʃɛ'rɛʃnʲa]
melon	диня (ж)	['dinʲa]

grapefruit	грейпфрут (ч)	[ɦrɛjp'frut]
avocado	авокадо (с)	[awo'kado]
papaya	папайя (ж)	[pa'paʲa]
mango	манго (с)	['manɦo]
pomegranate	гранат (ч)	[ɦra'nat]

redcurrant	порічки (мн)	[po'ritʃki]
blackcurrant	чорна смородина (ж)	['tʃɔrna smo'rɔdina]
gooseberry	аґрус (ч)	['agrus]
bilberry	чорниця (ж)	[tʃor'nitsʲa]
blackberry	ожина (ж)	[o'ʒina]
raisin	родзинки (мн)	[ro'dzinki]
fig	інжир (ч)	[in'ʒir]
date	фінік (ч)	['finik]
peanut	арахіс (ч)	[a'rahis]
almond	мигдаль (ч)	[miɦ'dalʲ]
walnut	горіх (ч) волоський	[ɦo'rih wo'lɔsʲkij]
hazelnut	ліщина (ж)	[li'ɕina]
coconut	горіх (ч) кокосовий	[ɦo'rih ko'kɔsowij]
pistachios	фісташки (мн)	[fis'taʃki]

56. Bread. Candy

bakers' confectionery (pastry)	кондитерські вироби (мн)	[kon'ditɛrsʲki 'wirobi]
bread	хліб (ч)	[hlib]
cookies	печиво (с)	['pɛtʃiwo]
chocolate (n)	шоколад (ч)	[ʃoko'lad]
chocolate (as adj)	шоколадний	[ʃoko'ladnij]
candy (wrapped)	цукерка (ж)	[tsu'kɛrka]
cake (e.g., cupcake)	тістечко (с)	['tistɛtʃko]
cake (e.g., birthday ~)	торт (ч)	[tort]
pie (e.g., apple ~)	пиріг (ч)	[pi'rih]
filling (for cake, pie)	начинка (ж)	[na'tʃinka]
jam (whole fruit jam)	варення (с)	[wa'rɛnʲa]
marmalade	мармелад (ч)	[marmɛ'lad]
waffles	вафлі (мн)	['wafli]
ice-cream	морозиво (с)	[mo'rɔziwo]

57. Spices

salt	сіль (ж)	[silʲ]
salty (adj)	солоний	[so'lɔnij]
to salt (vt)	солити	[so'liti]
black pepper	чорний перець (ч)	['tʃɔrnij 'pɛrɛts]
red pepper (milled ~)	червоний перець (ч)	[tʃɛr'wɔnij 'pɛrɛts]
mustard	гірчиця (ж)	[hir'tʃitsʲa]
horseradish	хрін (ч)	[hrin]

condiment	приправа (ж)	[priр'rawa]
spice	прянощі (мн)	[prʲa'nɔɕi]
sauce	соус (ч)	['sɔus]
vinegar	оцет (ч)	['ɔtsɛt]

anise	аніс (ч)	['anis]
basil	базилік (ч)	[bazi'lik]
cloves	гвоздика (ж)	[ɦwoz'dika]
ginger	імбир (ч)	[im'bir]
coriander	коріандр (ч)	[kori'andr]
cinnamon	кориця (ж)	[ko'ritsʲa]

sesame	кунжут (ч)	[kun'ʒut]
bay leaf	лавровий лист (ч)	[law'rɔwij list]
paprika	паприка (ж)	['paprika]
caraway	кмин (ч)	[kmin]
saffron	шафран (ч)	[ʃaf'ran]

PERSONAL
INFORMATION. FAMILY

T&P Books Publishing

58. Personal information. Forms

name (first name)	ім'я (c)	[i'm^ʲa]
surname (last name)	прізвище (c)	['prizwиɕɛ]
date of birth	дата (ж) народження	['data na'rɔdʑɛnʲa]
place of birth	місце (c) народження	['mistsɛ na'rɔdʑɛnʲa]
nationality	національність (ж)	[natsio'nalʲnistʲ]
place of residence	місце (c) проживання	['mistsɛ proʒi'wanʲa]
country	країна (ж)	[kra'jina]
profession (occupation)	професія (ж)	[pro'fɛsiʲa]
gender, sex	стать (ж)	[statʲ]
height	зріст (ч)	[zrist]
weight	вага (ж)	[wa'ɦa]

59. Family members. Relatives

mother	мати (ж)	['matи]
father	батько (ч)	['batʲko]
son	син (ч)	[sin]
daughter	дочка (ж)	[dotʃ'ka]
younger daughter	молодша дочка (ж)	[mo'lɔdʃa dotʃ'ka]
younger son	молодший син (ч)	[mo'lɔdʃij sin]
eldest daughter	старша дочка (ж)	['starʃa dotʃ'ka]
eldest son	старший син (ч)	['starʃij sin]
brother	брат (ч)	[brat]
sister	сестра (ж)	[sɛst'ra]
cousin (masc.)	двоюрідний брат (ч)	[dwoʲu'ridnij brat]
cousin (fem.)	двоюрідна сестра (ж)	[dwoʲu'ridna sɛst'ra]
mom, mommy	мати (ж)	['matи]
dad, daddy	тато (ч)	['tato]
parents	батьки (мн)	[batʲ'ki]
child	дитина (ж)	[di'tина]
children	діти (мн)	['diti]
grandmother	бабуся (ж)	[ba'busʲa]
grandfather	дід (ч)	['did]
grandson	онук (ч)	[o'nuk]
granddaughter	онука (ж)	[o'nuka]
grandchildren	онуки (мн)	[o'nuki]

uncle	дядько (ч)	['dʲadʲko]
aunt	тітка (ж)	['titka]
nephew	племінник (ч)	[plɛ'minik]
niece	племінниця (ж)	[plɛ'minitsʲa]

mother-in-law (wife's mother)	теща (ж)	['tɛɕa]
father-in-law (husband's father)	свекор (ч)	['swɛkor]
son-in-law (daughter's husband)	зять (ч)	[zʲatʲ]
stepmother	мачуха (ж)	['matʃuha]
stepfather	вітчим (ч)	['witʃim]

infant	немовля (с)	[nɛmow'lʲa]
baby (infant)	немовля (с)	[nɛmow'lʲa]
little boy, kid	малюк (ч)	[ma'lʲuk]

wife	дружина (ж)	[dru'ʒina]
husband	чоловік (ч)	[tʃolo'wik]
spouse (husband)	чоловік (ч)	[tʃolo'wik]
spouse (wife)	дружина (ж)	[dru'ʒina]

married (masc.)	одружений	[od'ruʒɛnij]
married (fem.)	заміжня	[za'miʒnʲa]
single (unmarried)	холостий	[holos'tij]
bachelor	холостяк (ч)	[holos'tʲak]
divorced (masc.)	розведений	[roz'wɛdɛnij]
widow	вдова (ж)	[wdo'wa]
widower	вдівець (ч)	[wdi'wɛts]

relative	родич (ч)	['rɔditʃ]
close relative	близький родич (ч)	[bliz'ʲkij 'rɔditʃ]
distant relative	далекий родич (ч)	[da'lɛkij 'rɔditʃ]
relatives	рідні (мн)	['ridni]

orphan (boy or girl)	сирота (ч)	[siro'ta]
guardian (of a minor)	опікун (ч)	[opi'kun]
to adopt (a boy)	усиновити	[usino'witi]
to adopt (a girl)	удочерити	[udotʃɛ'riti]

60. Friends. Coworkers

friend (masc.)	товариш (ч)	[to'wariʃ]
friend (fem.)	подруга (ж)	['podruha]
friendship	дружба (ж)	['druʒba]
to be friends	дружити	[dru'ʒiti]

buddy (masc.)	приятель (ч)	['prijatɛlʲ]
buddy (fem.)	приятелька (ж)	['prijatɛlʲka]

partner	**партнер** (ч)	[part'nɛr]
chief (boss)	**шеф** (ч)	[ʃɛf]
superior (n)	**начальник** (ч)	[na'tʃalʲnik]
subordinate (n)	**підлеглий** (ч)	[pid'lɛɦlij]
colleague	**колега** (ч)	[ko'lɛɦa]
acquaintance (person)	**знайомий** (ч)	[zna'jɔmij]
fellow traveler	**попутник** (ч)	[po'putnik]
classmate	**однокласник** (ч)	[odno'klasnik]
neighbor (masc.)	**сусід** (ч)	[su'sid]
neighbor (fem.)	**сусідка** (ж)	[su'sidka]
neighbors	**сусіди** (мн)	[su'sidi]

HUMAN BODY. MEDICINE

T&P Books Publishing

head	голова (ж)	[ɦoloˈwa]
face	обличчя (с)	[obˈlitʃʲa]
nose	ніс (ч)	[nis]
mouth	рот (ч)	[rot]
eye	око (с)	[ˈɔko]
eyes	очі (мн)	[ˈɔtʃi]
pupil	зіниця (ч)	[ziˈnitsʲa]
eyebrow	брова (ж)	[broˈwa]
eyelash	вія (ж)	[ˈwiʲa]
eyelid	повіка (ж)	[poˈwika]
tongue	язик (ч)	[jaˈzɨk]
tooth	зуб (ч)	[zub]
lips	губи (мн)	[ˈɦubɨ]
cheekbones	вилиці (мн)	[ˈwilɨtsi]
gum	ясна (мн)	[ˈʲasna]
palate	піднебіння (с)	[pidnɛˈbinʲa]
nostrils	ніздрі (мн)	[ˈnizdri]
chin	підборіддя (с)	[pidboˈriddʲa]
jaw	щелепа (ж)	[ɕɛˈlɛpa]
cheek	щока (ж)	[ɕoˈka]
forehead	чоло (с)	[tʃoˈlɔ]
temple	скроня (ж)	[ˈskrɔnʲa]
ear	вухо (с)	[ˈwuho]
back of the head	потилиця (ж)	[poˈtilɨtsʲa]
neck	шия (ж)	[ˈʃiʲa]
throat	горло (с)	[ˈɦɔrlo]
hair	волосся (с)	[woˈlɔssʲa]
hairstyle	зачіска (ж)	[ˈzatʃiska]
haircut	стрижка (ж)	[ˈstriʒka]
wig	парик (ч)	[paˈrik]
mustache	вуса (мн)	[ˈwusa]
beard	борода (ж)	[boroˈda]
to have (a beard, etc.)	носити	[noˈsiti]
braid	коса (ж)	[koˈsa]
sideburns	бакенбарди (мн)	[bakɛnˈbardi]
red-haired (adj)	рудий	[ruˈdij]
gray (hair)	сивий	[ˈsiwij]

| bald (adj) | лисий | ['lisij] |
| bald patch | лисина (ж) | ['lisina] |

| ponytail | хвіст (ч) | [hwist] |
| bangs | чубчик (ч) | ['tʃubtʃik] |

62. Human body

| hand | кисть (ж) | [kistʲ] |
| arm | рука (ж) | [ru'ka] |

finger	палець (ч)	['palɛts]
thumb	великий палець (ч)	[wɛ'likij 'palɛts]
little finger	мізинець (ч)	[mi'zinɛts]
nail	ніготь (ч)	['niɦotʲ]

fist	кулак (ч)	[ku'lak]
palm	долоня (ж)	[do'lɔnʲa]
wrist	зап'ясток (ч)	[za'pʲʲastok]
forearm	передпліччя (с)	[pɛrɛdp'litʃʲa]
elbow	лікоть (ч)	['likotʲ]
shoulder	плече (с)	[plɛ'tʃɛ]

leg	гомілка (ж)	[ɦo'milka]
foot	ступня (ж)	[stup'nʲa]
knee	коліно (с)	[ko'lino]
calf (part of leg)	литка (ж)	['litka]

| hip | стегно (с) | [stɛɦ'nɔ] |
| heel | п'ятка (ж) | ['pʲʲatka] |

body	тіло (с)	['tilo]
stomach	живіт (ч)	[ʒi'wit]
chest	груди (мн)	['ɦrudi]
breast	груди (мн)	['ɦrudi]

flank	бік (ч)	[bik]
back	спина (ж)	['spina]
lower back	поперек (ч)	[popɛ'rɛk]
waist	талія (ж)	['taliʲa]

navel (belly button)	пупок (ч)	[pu'pɔk]
buttocks	сідниці (мн)	[sid'nitsi]
bottom	зад (ч)	[zad]

beauty mark	родимка (ж)	['rɔdimka]
birthmark (café au lait spot)	родима пляма (ж)	[ro'dima 'plʲama]
tattoo	татуювання (с)	[tatuʲu'wanʲa]
scar	рубець (ч)	[ru'bɛts]

63. Diseases

sickness	хвороба (ж)	[hwo'rɔba]
to be sick	хворіти	[hwo'riti]
health	здоров'я (с)	[zdo'rɔwʲa]

runny nose (coryza)	нежить (ч)	['nɛʒitʲ]
tonsillitis	ангіна (ж)	[an'ɦina]
cold (illness)	застуда (ж)	[za'studa]
to catch a cold	застудитися	[zastu'ditisʲa]

bronchitis	бронхіт (ч)	[bron'hit]
pneumonia	запалення (с) легенів	[za'palɛnja lɛ'ɦɛniw]
flu, influenza	грип (ч)	[ɦrip]

nearsighted (adj)	короткозорий	[korotko'zɔrij]
farsighted (adj)	далекозорий	[dalɛko'zɔrij]
strabismus (crossed eyes)	косоокість (ж)	[koso'ɔkistʲ]
cross-eyed (adj)	косоокий	[koso'ɔkij]
cataract	катаракта (ж)	[kata'rakta]
glaucoma	глаукома (ж)	[ɦlau'kɔma]

stroke	інсульт (ч)	[in'sulʲt]
heart attack	інфаркт (ч)	[in'farkt]
myocardial infarction	інфаркт (ч) міокарду	[in'farkt mio'kardu]
paralysis	параліч (ч)	[para'litʲ]
to paralyze (vt)	паралізувати	[paralizu'wati]

allergy	алергія (ж)	[alɛr'ɦiʲa]
asthma	астма (ж)	['astma]
diabetes	діабет (ч)	[dia'bɛt]

toothache	зубний біль (ч)	[zub'nij bilʲ]
caries	карієс (ч)	['kariɛs]

diarrhea	діарея (ж)	[dia'rɛʲa]
constipation	запор (ч)	[za'pɔr]
stomach upset	розлад (ч) шлунку	['rɔzlad 'ʃlunku]
food poisoning	отруєння (с)	[ot'ruɛnʲa]
to get food poisoning	отруїтись	[otru'jitisʲ]

arthritis	артрит (ч)	[art'rit]
rickets	рахіт (ч)	[ra'hit]
rheumatism	ревматизм (ч)	[rɛwma'tizm]
atherosclerosis	атеросклероз (ч)	[atɛrosklɛ'rɔz]

gastritis	гастрит (ч)	[ɦast'rit]
appendicitis	апендицит (ч)	[apɛndi'tsit]
cholecystitis	холецистит (ч)	[holɛtsis'tit]
ulcer	виразка (ж)	['wirazka]
measles	кір (ч)	[kir]

rubella (German measles)	краснуха (ж)	[kras'nuha]
jaundice	жовтуха (ж)	[ʒow'tuha]
hepatitis	гепатит (ч)	[hɛpa'tit]

schizophrenia	шизофренія (ж)	[ʃizofrɛ'niʲa]
rabies (hydrophobia)	сказ (ч)	[skaz]
neurosis	невроз (ч)	[nɛw'rɔz]
concussion	струс (ч) мозку	['strus 'mɔzku]

cancer	рак (ч)	[rak]
sclerosis	склероз (ч)	[sklɛ'rɔz]
multiple sclerosis	розсіяний склероз (ч)	[roz'siʲanij sklɛ'rɔz]

alcoholism	алкоголізм (ч)	[alkoho'lizm]
alcoholic (n)	алкоголік (ч)	[alko'hɔlik]
syphilis	сифіліс (ч)	['sifilis]
AIDS	СНІД (ч)	[snid]

tumor	пухлина (ж)	[puh'lɨna]
malignant (adj)	злоякісна	[zlo'ʲakisna]
benign (adj)	доброякісний	[dobro'ʲakisnij]

fever	гарячка (ж)	[ha'rʲatʃka]
malaria	малярія (ж)	[malʲa'riʲa]
gangrene	гангрена (ж)	[han'hrɛna]
seasickness	морська хвороба (ж)	[morsʲ'ka hwo'rɔba]
epilepsy	епілепсія (ж)	[ɛpi'lɛpsiʲa]

epidemic	епідемія (ж)	[ɛpi'dɛmiʲa]
typhus	тиф (ч)	[tif]
tuberculosis	туберкульоз (ч)	[tubɛrku'lʲoz]
cholera	холера (ж)	[ho'lɛra]
plague (bubonic ~)	чума (ж)	[tʃu'ma]

64. Symptoms. Treatments. Part 1

symptom	симптом (ч)	[sɨmp'tɔm]
temperature	температура (ж)	[tɛmpɛra'tura]
high temperature (fever)	висока температура (ж)	[wi'sɔka tɛmpɛra'tura]
pulse	пульс (ч)	[pulʲs]

dizziness (vertigo)	запаморочення (с)	[za'pamorotʃɛnʲa]
hot (adj)	гарячий	[ha'rʲatʃij]
shivering	озноб (ч)	[oz'nɔb]
pale (e.g., ~ face)	блідий	[bli'dij]

cough	кашель (ч)	['kaʃɛlʲ]
to cough (vi)	кашляти	['kaʃlʲati]
to sneeze (vi)	чхати	['tʃhati]
faint	непритомність (ж)	[nɛpri'tɔmnistʲ]

to faint (vi)	знепритомніти	[znɛpri'tɔmniti]
bruise (hématome)	синець (ч)	[si'nɛts]
bump (lump)	гуля (ж)	['ɦulʲa]
to bang (bump)	ударитись	[u'daritisʲ]
contusion (bruise)	забите місце (с)	[za'bitɛ 'mistsɛ]
to get a bruise	забитися	[za'bitisʲa]
to limp (vi)	кульгати	[kulʲ'ɦati]
dislocation	вивих (ч)	['wiwiɦ]
to dislocate (vt)	вивихнути	['wiwiɦnuti]
fracture	перелом (ч)	[pɛrɛ'lɔm]
to have a fracture	дістати перелом	[dis'tati pɛrɛ'lɔm]
cut (e.g., paper ~)	поріз (ч)	[po'riz]
to cut oneself	порізатися	[po'rizatisʲa]
bleeding	кровотеча (ж)	[krowo'tɛtʃa]
burn (injury)	опік (ч)	['ɔpik]
to get burned	обпектися	[obpɛk'tisʲa]
to prick (vt)	уколоти	[uko'lɔti]
to prick oneself	уколотися	[uko'lɔtisʲa]
to injure (vt)	пошкодити	[poʃ'kɔditi]
injury	ушкодження (с)	[uʃ'kɔdʑɛnʲa]
wound	рана (ж)	['rana]
trauma	травма (ж)	['trawma]
to be delirious	марити	['mariti]
to stutter (vi)	заїкатися	[zajі'katisʲa]
sunstroke	сонячний удар (ч)	['sɔnʲatʃnij u'dar]

65. Symptoms. Treatments. Part 2

pain, ache	біль (ч)	[bilʲ]
splinter (in foot, etc.)	скалка (ж)	['skalka]
sweat (perspiration)	піт (ч)	[pit]
to sweat (perspire)	спітніти	[spit'niti]
vomiting	блювота (ж)	[blʲu'wɔta]
convulsions	судома (ж)	[su'dɔma]
pregnant (adj)	вагітна	[wa'ɦitna]
to be born	народитися	[naro'ditisʲa]
delivery, labor	пологи (мн)	[po'lɔɦi]
to deliver (~ a baby)	народжувати	[na'rɔdʑuwati]
abortion	аборт (ч)	[a'bɔrt]
breathing, respiration	дихання (с)	['diɦanʲa]
in-breath (inhalation)	вдих (ч)	[wdiɦ]
out-breath (exhalation)	видих (ч)	['widiɦ]

| to exhale (breathe out) | видихнути | ['wɨdɨhnutɨ] |
| to inhale (vi) | зробити вдих | [zro'bɨtɨ wdɨh] |

disabled person	інвалід (ч)	[inwa'lid]
cripple	каліка (ч)	[ka'lika]
drug addict	наркоман (ч)	[narko'man]

deaf (adj)	глухий (ч)	[ɦlu'hɨj]
mute (adj)	німий (ч)	[ni'mɨj]
deaf mute (adj)	глухонімий (ч)	[ɦluhoni'mɨj]

mad, insane (adj)	божевільний	[boʒɛ'wilʲnɨj]
madman (demented person)	божевільний (ч)	[boʒɛ'wilʲnɨj]
madwoman	божевільна (ж)	[boʒɛ'wilʲna]
to go insane	збожеволіти	[zboʒɛ'wɔlitɨ]

gene	ген (ч)	[ɦɛn]
immunity	імунітет (ч)	[imuni'tɛt]
hereditary (adj)	спадковий	[spad'kɔwɨj]
congenital (adj)	вроджений	['wrɔdʒɛnɨj]

virus	вірус (ч)	['wirus]
microbe	мікроб (ч)	[mik'rɔb]
bacterium	бактерія (ж)	[bak'tɛriʲa]
infection	інфекція (ж)	[in'fɛkʦiʲa]

66. Symptoms. Treatments. Part 3

| hospital | лікарня (ж) | [li'karnʲa] |
| patient | пацієнт (ч) | [paʦi'ɛnt] |

diagnosis	діагноз (ч)	[di'aɦnoz]
cure	лікування (с)	[liku'wanʲa]
medical treatment	лікування (с)	[liku'wanʲa]
to get treatment	лікуватися	[liku'watisʲa]
to treat (~ a patient)	лікувати	[liku'watɨ]
to nurse (look after)	доглядати	[doɦlʲa'datɨ]
care (nursing ~)	догляд (ч)	['dɔɦlʲad]

operation, surgery	операція (ж)	[opɛ'raʦiʲa]
to bandage (head, limb)	перев'язати	[pɛrɛw'ʲa'zatɨ]
bandaging	перев'язка (ж)	[pɛrɛ'w'ʲazka]

vaccination	щеплення (с)	['ɕɛplɛnʲa]
to vaccinate (vt)	робити щеплення	[ro'bɨtɨ 'ɕɛplɛnʲa]
injection, shot	ін'єкція (ж)	[i'n'ɛkʦiʲa]
to give an injection	робити укол	[ro'bɨtɨ u'kɔl]
amputation	ампутація (ж)	[ampu'taʦiʲa]
to amputate (vt)	ампутувати	[amputu'watɨ]

coma	кома (ж)	['kɔma]
to be in a coma	бути в комі	['buti w 'kɔmi]
intensive care	реанімація (ж)	[rɛaniˈmatsiʲa]

to recover (~ from flu)	видужувати	[wiˈduʒuwati]
condition (patient's ~)	стан (ч)	['stan]
consciousness	свідомість (ж)	[swiˈdɔmistʲ]
memory (faculty)	пам'ять (ж)	['pamʲatʲ]

to pull out (tooth)	видалити	['widaliti]
filling	пломба (ж)	['plɔmba]
to fill (a tooth)	пломбувати	[plombuˈwati]

| hypnosis | гіпноз (ч) | [hipˈnɔz] |
| to hypnotize (vt) | гіпнотизувати | [hipnotizuˈwati] |

67. Medicine. Drugs. Accessories

medicine, drug	ліки (мн)	['liki]
remedy	засіб (ч)	['zasib]
to prescribe (vt)	прописати	[propiˈsati]
prescription	рецепт (ч)	[rɛˈtsɛpt]

tablet, pill	пігулка (ж)	[piˈhulka]
ointment	мазь (ж)	[mazʲ]
ampule	ампула (ж)	['ampula]
mixture	мікстура (ж)	[miksˈtura]
syrup	сироп (ч)	[siˈrɔp]
pill	пілюля (ж)	[piˈlʲulʲa]
powder	порошок (ч)	[poroˈʃɔk]

gauze bandage	бинт (ч)	[bint]
cotton wool	вата (ж)	['wata]
iodine	йод (ч)	[ˈʲod]

Band-Aid	лейкопластир (ч)	[lɛjkoˈplastir]
eyedropper	піпетка (ж)	[piˈpɛtka]
thermometer	градусник (ч)	['hradusnik]
syringe	шприц (ч)	[ʃprits]

| wheelchair | коляска (ж) | [koˈlʲaska] |
| crutches | милиці (мн) | ['militsi] |

painkiller	знеболювальне (с)	[znɛˈbolʲuwalʲnɛ]
laxative	проносне (с)	[pronosˈnɛ]
spirits (ethanol)	спирт (ч)	[spirt]
medicinal herbs	трава (ж)	[traˈwa]
herbal (~ tea)	трав'яний	[trawʲaˈnij]

APARTMENT

T&P Books Publishing

68. Apartment

apartment	квартира (ж)	[kwar'tira]
room	кімната (ж)	[kim'nata]
bedroom	спальня (ж)	['spalʲnʲa]
dining room	їдальня (ж)	['jɨdalʲnʲa]
living room	вітальня (ж)	[wi'talʲnʲa]
study (home office)	кабінет (ч)	[kabi'nɛt]

entry room	передпокій (ч)	[pɛrɛd'pɔkij]
bathroom (room with a bath or shower)	ванна кімната (ж)	['waɲa kim'nata]
half bath	туалет (ч)	[tua'lɛt]

ceiling	стеля (ж)	['stɛlʲa]
floor	підлога (ж)	[pid'lɔɦa]
corner	куток (ч)	[ku'tɔk]

69. Furniture. Interior

furniture	меблі (мн)	['mɛbli]
table	стіл (ч)	[stil]
chair	стілець (ч)	[sti'lɛts]
bed	ліжко (с)	['liʒko]
couch, sofa	диван (ч)	[di'wan]
armchair	крісло (с)	['krislo]

| bookcase | шафа (ж) | ['ʃafa] |
| shelf | полиця (ж) | [po'litsʲa] |

wardrobe	шафа (ж)	['ʃafa]
coat rack (wall-mounted ~)	вішалка (ж)	['wiʃalka]
coat stand	вішак (ч)	[wi'ʃak]

| bureau, dresser | комод (ч) | [ko'mɔd] |
| coffee table | журнальний столик (ч) | [ʒur'nalʲnij 'stɔlik] |

mirror	дзеркало (с)	['dzɛrkalo]
carpet	килим (ч)	['kilim]
rug, small carpet	килимок (ч)	[kili'mɔk]

fireplace	камін (ч)	[ka'min]
candle	свічка (ж)	['switʃka]
candlestick	свічник (ч)	[switʃ'nik]

drapes	штори (мн)	['ʃtɔri]
wallpaper	шпалери (мн)	[ʃpa'lɛri]
blinds (jalousie)	жалюзі (мн)	['ʒalʲuzi]

table lamp	настільна лампа (ж)	[na'stilʲna 'lampa]
wall lamp (sconce)	світильник (ч)	[swi'tilʲnik]
floor lamp	торшер (ч)	[tor'ʃɛr]
chandelier	люстра (ж)	['lʲustra]

leg (of chair, table)	ніжка (ж)	['niʒka]
armrest	підлокітник (ч)	[pidlo'kitnik]
back (backrest)	спинка (ж)	['spinka]
drawer	шухляда (ж)	[ʃuh'lʲada]

70. Bedding

bedclothes	білизна (ж)	[bi'lizna]
pillow	подушка (ж)	[po'duʃka]
pillowcase	наволочка (ж)	['nawolotʃka]
duvet, comforter	ковдра (ж)	['kɔwdra]
sheet	простирадло (с)	[prosti'radlo]
bedspread	покривало (с)	[pokri'walo]

71. Kitchen

kitchen	кухня (ж)	['kuhnʲa]
gas	газ (ч)	[ɦaz]
gas stove (range)	плита (ж) газова	[pli'ta 'ɦazowa]
electric stove	плита (ж) електрична	[pli'ta ɛlɛkt'ritʃna]
oven	духовка (ж)	[du'hɔwka]
microwave oven	мікрохвильова піч (ж)	[mikrohwilʲo'wa pitʃ]

refrigerator	холодильник (ч)	[holo'dilʲnik]
freezer	морозильник (ч)	[moro'zilʲnik]
dishwasher	посудомийна машина (ж)	[posudo'mijna ma'ʃina]

meat grinder	м'ясорубка (ж)	[mʲaso'rubka]
juicer	соковижималка (ж)	[sokowiʒi'malka]
toaster	тостер (ч)	['tɔstɛr]
mixer	міксер (ч)	['miksɛr]
coffee machine	кавоварка (ж)	[kawo'warka]
coffee pot	кавник (ч)	[kaw'nik]
coffee grinder	кавомолка (ж)	[kawo'mɔlka]

kettle	чайник (ч)	['tʃajnik]
teapot	заварник (ч)	[za'warnik]
lid	кришка (ж)	['kriʃka]

tea strainer	ситечко (с)	['sitɛtʃko]
spoon	ложка (ж)	['lɔʒka]
teaspoon	чайна ложка (ж)	['tʃajna 'lɔʒka]
soup spoon	столова ложка (ж)	[sto'lɔwa 'lɔʒka]
fork	виделка (ж)	[wi'dɛlka]
knife	ніж (ч)	[niʒ]

tableware (dishes)	посуд (ч)	['pɔsud]
plate (dinner ~)	тарілка (ж)	[ta'rilka]
saucer	блюдце (с)	['blʲudtsɛ]

shot glass	чарка (ж)	['tʃarka]
glass (tumbler)	склянка (ж)	['sklʲanka]
cup	чашка (ж)	['tʃaʃka]

sugar bowl	цукорниця (ж)	['tsukornitsʲa]
salt shaker	сільничка (ж)	[silʲ'nitʃka]
pepper shaker	перечниця (ж)	['pɛrɛtʃnitsʲa]
butter dish	маслянка (ж)	['maslʲanka]

stock pot (soup pot)	каструля (ж)	[kas'trulʲa]
frying pan (skillet)	сковорідка (ж)	[skowo'ridka]
ladle	черпак (ч)	[tʃɛr'pak]
colander	друшляк (ч)	[druʃ'lʲak]
tray (serving ~)	піднос (ч)	[pid'nɔs]

bottle	пляшка (ж)	['plʲaʃka]
jar (glass)	банка (ж)	['banka]
can	банка (ж)	['banka]

bottle opener	відкривачка (ж)	[widkri'watʃka]
can opener	відкривачка (ж)	[widkri'watʃka]
corkscrew	штопор (ч)	['ʃtɔpor]
filter	фільтр (ч)	['filʲtr]
to filter (vt)	фільтрувати	[filʲtru'wati]

| trash, garbage (food waste, etc.) | сміття (с) | [smit'tʲa] |
| trash can (kitchen ~) | відро (с) для сміття | [wid'rɔ dlʲa smit'tʲa] |

72. Bathroom

bathroom	ванна кімната (ж)	['wana kim'nata]
water	вода (ж)	[wo'da]
faucet	кран (ч)	[kran]
hot water	гаряча вода (ж)	[ha'rʲatʃa wo'da]
cold water	холодна вода (ж)	[ho'lɔdna wo'da]

| toothpaste | зубна паста (ж) | [zub'na 'pasta] |
| to brush one's teeth | чистити зуби | ['tʃistiti 'zubi] |

to shave (vi)	голитися	[ɦoˈlitisʲa]
shaving foam	піна (ж) для гоління	[ˈpina dlʲa ɦoˈlinʲa]
razor	бритва (ж)	[ˈbritwa]

to wash (one's hands, etc.)	мити	[ˈmiti]
to take a bath	митися	[ˈmitisʲa]
shower	душ (ч)	[duʃ]
to take a shower	приймати душ	[prijˈmati duʃ]

bathtub	ванна (ж)	[ˈwana]
toilet (toilet bowl)	унітаз (ч)	[uniˈtaz]
sink (washbasin)	раковина (ж)	[ˈrakowina]

| soap | мило (с) | [ˈmilo] |
| soap dish | мильниця (ж) | [ˈmilʲnitsʲa] |

sponge	губка (ж)	[ˈɦubka]
shampoo	шампунь (ч)	[ʃamˈpunʲ]
towel	рушник (ч)	[ruʃˈnik]
bathrobe	халат (ч)	[haˈlat]

laundry (process)	прання (с)	[praˈnʲa]
washing machine	пральна машина (ж)	[ˈpralʲna maˈʃina]
to do the laundry	прати білизну	[ˈprati biˈliznu]
laundry detergent	пральний порошок (ч)	[ˈpralʲnij poroˈʃɔk]

73. Household appliances

TV set	телевізор (ч)	[tɛlɛˈwizor]
tape recorder	магнітофон (ч)	[maɦnitoˈfon]
VCR (video recorder)	відеомагнітофон (ч)	[ˈwidɛo maɦnitoˈfon]
radio	приймач (ч)	[prijˈmatʃ]
player (CD, MP3, etc.)	плеєр (ч)	[ˈplɛɛr]

video projector	відеопроектор (ч)	[ˈwidɛo proˈɛktor]
home movie theater	домашній кінотеатр (ч)	[doˈmaʃnij kinotɛˈatr]
DVD player	програвач (ч) DVD	[proɦraˈwatʃ diwiˈdi]
amplifier	підсилювач (ч)	[pidˈsilʲuwatʃ]
video game console	гральна приставка (ж)	[ˈɦralʲna priˈstawka]

video camera	відеокамера (ж)	[ˈwidɛo ˈkamɛra]
camera (photo)	фотоапарат (ч)	[fotoapaˈrat]
digital camera	цифровий фотоапарат (ч)	[tsifroˈwij fotoapaˈrat]

vacuum cleaner	пилосос (ч)	[piloˈsɔs]
iron (e.g., steam ~)	праска (ж)	[ˈpraska]
ironing board	дошка (ж) для прасування	[ˈdɔʃka dlʲa prasuˈwanʲa]

| telephone | телефон (ч) | [tɛlɛˈfon] |

cell phone	**мобільний телефон** (ч)	[mo'bilʲnɨj tɛlɛ'fɔn]
typewriter	**машинка** (ж)	[ma'ʃɨnka]
sewing machine	**швейна машинка** (ж)	['ʃwɛjna ma'ʃɨnka]
microphone	**мікрофон** (ч)	[mikro'fɔn]
headphones	**навушники** (мн)	[na'wuʃnɨkɨ]
remote control (TV)	**пульт** (ч)	[pulʲt]
CD, compact disc	**CD-диск** (ч)	[si'di dɨsk]
cassette, tape	**касета** (ж)	[ka'sɛta]
vinyl record	**платівка** (ж)	[pla'tiwka]

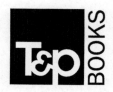

THE EARTH. WEATHER

T&P Books Publishing

space	космос (ч)	['kɔsmos]
space (as adj)	космічний	[kos'mitʃnij]
outer space	космічний простір (ч)	[kos'mitʃnij 'prɔstir]

universe	всесвіт (ч)	['wsɛswit]
galaxy	галактика (ж)	[ɦa'laktika]

star	зірка (ж)	['zirka]
constellation	сузір'я (с)	[su'zirʲa]
planet	планета (ж)	[pla'nɛta]
satellite	супутник (ч)	[su'putnɨk]

meteorite	метеорит (ч)	[mɛtɛo'rit]
comet	комета (ж)	[ko'mɛta]
asteroid	астероїд (ч)	[astɛ'rɔjid]

orbit	орбіта (ж)	[or'bita]
to revolve (~ around the Earth)	обертатися	[obɛr'tatisʲa]
atmosphere	атмосфера (ж)	[atmos'fɛra]

the Sun	Сонце (с)	['sɔntsɛ]
solar system	Сонячна система (ж)	['sɔnʲatʃna sɨs'tɛma]
solar eclipse	сонячне затемнення (с)	['sɔnʲatʃnɛ za'tɛmnɛnʲa]

the Earth	Земля (ж)	[zɛm'lʲa]
the Moon	Місяць (ж)	['misʲats]

Mars	Марс (ч)	[mars]
Venus	Венера (ж)	[wɛ'nɛra]
Jupiter	Юпітер (ч)	[ʲu'pitɛr]
Saturn	Сатурн (ч)	[sa'turn]

Mercury	Меркурій (ч)	[mɛr'kurij]
Uranus	Уран (ч)	[u'ran]
Neptune	Нептун (ч)	[nɛp'tun]
Pluto	Плутон (ч)	[plu'tɔn]

Milky Way	Чумацький Шлях (ч)	[tʃu'matskij ʃlʲah]
Great Bear (Ursa Major)	Велика Ведмедиця (ж)	[wɛ'lika wɛd'mɛditsʲa]
North Star	Полярна Зірка (ж)	[po'lʲarna 'zirka]

Martian	марсіанин (ч)	[marsi'anɨn]
extraterrestrial (n)	інопланетянин (ч)	[inoplanɛ'tʲanɨn]

| alien | прибулець (ч) | [priˈbulɛts] |
| flying saucer | літальна тарілка (ж) | [liˈtalʲna taˈrilka] |

spaceship	космічний корабель (ч)	[kosˈmitʃnij koraˈbɛlʲ]
space station	орбітальна станція (ж)	[orbiˈtalʲna ˈstantsiʲa]
blast-off	старт (ч)	[start]

engine	двигун (ч)	[dwiˈɦun]
nozzle	сопло (с)	[ˈsɔplo]
fuel	паливо (с)	[ˈpaliwo]

cockpit, flight deck	кабіна (ж)	[kaˈbina]
antenna	антена (ж)	[anˈtɛna]
porthole	ілюмінатор (ч)	[ilʲumiˈnator]
solar panel	сонячна батарея (ж)	[ˈsɔnʲatʃna bataˈrɛʲa]
spacesuit	скафандр (ч)	[skaˈfandr]

| weightlessness | невагомість (ж) | [nɛwaˈɦomistʲ] |
| oxygen | кисень (ч) | [ˈkisɛnʲ] |

| docking (in space) | стикування (с) | [stikuˈwanʲa] |
| to dock (vi, vt) | здійснювати стикування | [ˈzdijsnʲuwati stikuˈwanʲa] |

observatory	обсерваторія (ж)	[obsɛrwaˈtoriʲa]
telescope	телескоп (ч)	[tɛlɛˈskɔp]
to observe (vt)	спостерігати	[spostɛriˈɦati]
to explore (vt)	досліджувати	[doˈslidʒuwati]

75. The Earth

the Earth	Земля (ж)	[zɛmˈlʲa]
the globe (the Earth)	земна куля (ж)	[zɛmˈna ˈkulʲa]
planet	планета (ж)	[plaˈnɛta]

atmosphere	атмосфера (ж)	[atmosˈfɛra]
geography	географія (ж)	[ɦɛoˈɦrafiʲa]
nature	природа (ж)	[priˈrɔda]

globe (table ~)	глобус (ч)	[ˈɦlɔbus]
map	карта (ж)	[ˈkarta]
atlas	атлас (ч)	[ˈatlas]

Europe	Європа (ж)	[ɛwˈrɔpa]
Asia	Азія (ж)	[ˈaziʲa]
Africa	Африка (ж)	[ˈafrika]
Australia	Австралія (ж)	[awˈstraliʲa]

| America | Америка (ж) | [aˈmɛrika] |
| North America | Північна Америка (ж) | [piwˈnitʃna aˈmɛrika] |

South America	Південна Америка (ж)	[piw'dɛna a'mɛrika]
Antarctica	Антарктида (ж)	[antark'tida]
the Arctic	Арктика (ж)	['arktika]

76. Cardinal directions

north	північ (ж)	['piwnitʃ]
to the north	на північ	[na 'piwnitʃ]
in the north	на півночі	[na 'piwnotʃi]
northern (adj)	північний	[piw'nitʃnij]

south	південь (ч)	['piwdɛnʲ]
to the south	на південь	[na 'piwdɛnʲ]
in the south	на півдні	[na 'piwdni]
southern (adj)	південний	[piw'dɛnij]

west	захід (ч)	['zahid]
to the west	на захід	[na 'zahid]
in the west	на заході	[na 'zahodi]
western (adj)	західний	['zahidnij]

east	схід (ч)	[shid]
to the east	на схід	[na 'shid]
in the east	на сході	[na 'shɔdi]
eastern (adj)	східний	['shidnij]

77. Sea. Ocean

sea	море (с)	['mɔrɛ]
ocean	океан (ч)	[okɛ'an]
gulf (bay)	затока (ж)	[za'tɔka]
straits	протока (ж)	[pro'tɔka]

continent (mainland)	материк (ч)	[matɛ'rik]
island	острів (ч)	['ɔstriw]
peninsula	півострів (ч)	[pi'wɔstriw]
archipelago	архіпелаг (ч)	[arhipɛ'laɦ]

bay, cove	бухта (ж)	['buhta]
harbor	гавань (ж)	['ɦawanʲ]
lagoon	лагуна (ж)	[la'ɦuna]
cape	мис (ч)	[mis]

atoll	атол (ч)	[a'tɔl]
reef	риф (ч)	[rif]
coral	корал (ч)	[ko'ral]
coral reef	кораловий риф (ч)	[ko'ralowij rif]
deep (adj)	глибокий	[ɦli'bɔkij]

depth (deep water)	глибина (ж)	[ɦlibi'na]
abyss	безодня (ж)	['bɛzdna]
trench (e.g., Mariana ~)	западина (ж)	[za'padina]

current (Ocean ~)	течія (ж)	['tɛtʃiʲa]
to surround (bathe)	омивати	[omɨ'wati]

shore	берег (ч)	['bɛrɛɦ]
coast	узбережжя (с)	[uzbɛ'rɛʑʲa]

flow (flood tide)	приплив (ч)	[prɨp'liw]
ebb (ebb tide)	відплив (ч)	[wid'pliw]
shoal	обмілина (ж)	[ob'milina]
bottom (~ of the sea)	дно (с)	[dno]

wave	хвиля (ж)	['hwilʲa]
crest (~ of a wave)	гребінь (ч) хвилі	['ɦrɛbinʲ 'hwili]
spume (sea foam)	піна (ж)	[pi'na]

storm (sea storm)	буря (ж)	['burʲa]
hurricane	ураган (ч)	[uraɦan]
tsunami	цунамі (с)	[ʦu'nami]
calm (dead ~)	штиль (ч)	[ʃtilʲ]
quiet, calm (adj)	спокійний	[spo'kijnij]

pole	полюс (ч)	['polʲus]
polar (adj)	полярний	[po'lʲarnij]

latitude	широта (ж)	[ʃiro'ta]
longitude	довгота (ж)	[dowɦo'ta]
parallel	паралель (ж)	[para'lɛlʲ]
equator	екватор (ч)	[ɛk'wator]

sky	небо (с)	['nɛbo]
horizon	горизонт (ч)	[ɦorɨ'zɔnt]
air	повітря (с)	[po'witrʲa]

lighthouse	маяк (ч)	[ma'ʲak]
to dive (vi)	пірнати	[pir'nati]
to sink (ab. boat)	затонути	[zato'nuti]
treasures	скарби (мн)	[skar'bi]

78. Seas' and Oceans' names

Atlantic Ocean	Атлантичний океан (ч)	[atlan'titʃnij okɛ'an]
Indian Ocean	Індійський океан (ч)	[in'dijsʲkij okɛ'an]
Pacific Ocean	Тихий океан (ч)	['tihij okɛ'an]
Arctic Ocean	Північний Льодовитий океан (ч)	[piw'nitʃnij lʲodo'witij okɛ'an]
Black Sea	Чорне море (с)	['tʃɔrnɛ 'mɔrɛ]

Red Sea	Червоне море (c)	[tʃɛr'wɔnɛ 'mɔrɛ]
Yellow Sea	Жовте море (c)	['ʒɔwtɛ 'mɔrɛ]
White Sea	Біле море (c)	['bilɛ 'mɔrɛ]

Caspian Sea	Каспійське море (c)	[kas'pijsʲkɛ 'mɔrɛ]
Dead Sea	Мертве море (c)	['mɛrtwɛ 'mɔrɛ]
Mediterranean Sea	Середземне море (c)	[sɛrɛ'dzɛmnɛ 'mɔrɛ]

| Aegean Sea | Егейське море (c) | [ɛ'ɦɛjsʲkɛ 'mɔrɛ] |
| Adriatic Sea | Адріатичне море (c) | [adria'titʃnɛ 'mɔrɛ] |

Arabian Sea	Аравійське море (c)	[ara'wijsʲkɛ 'mɔrɛ]
Sea of Japan	Японське море (c)	[ja'pɔnsʲkɛ 'mɔrɛ]
Bering Sea	Берингове море (c)	['bɛrinɦɔwɛ 'mɔrɛ]
South China Sea	Південно-Китайське море (c)	[piw'dɛnɔ ki'tajsʲkɛ 'mɔrɛ]

Coral Sea	Коралове море (c)	[ko'ralɔwɛ 'mɔrɛ]
Tasman Sea	Тасманове море (c)	[tas'manɔwɛ 'mɔrɛ]
Caribbean Sea	Карибське море (c)	[ka'ribsʲkɛ 'mɔrɛ]

| Barents Sea | Баренцове море (c) | ['barɛntsɔwɛ 'mɔrɛ] |
| Kara Sea | Карське море (c) | ['karsʲkɛ 'mɔrɛ] |

North Sea	Північне море (c)	[piw'nitʃnɛ 'mɔrɛ]
Baltic Sea	Балтійське море (c)	[bal'tijsʲkɛ 'mɔrɛ]
Norwegian Sea	Норвезьке море (c)	[nor'wɛzʲkɛ 'mɔrɛ]

79. Mountains

mountain	гора (ж)	[ɦo'ra]
mountain range	гірське пасмо (c)	[ɦirsʲ'kɛ 'pasmo]
mountain ridge	гірський хребет (ч)	[ɦirsʲ'kij ɦrɛ'bɛt]

summit, top	вершина (ж)	[wɛr'ʃina]
peak	шпиль (ч)	[ʃpilʲ]
foot (~ of the mountain)	підніжжя (c)	[pid'niʒʲa]
slope (mountainside)	схил (ч)	[sɦil]

volcano	вулкан (ч)	[wul'kan]
active volcano	діючий вулкан (ч)	['diʲutʃij wul'kan]
dormant volcano	згаслий вулкан (ч)	['zɦaslij wul'kan]

eruption	виверження (c)	['wiwɛrʒɛnʲa]
crater	кратер (ч)	['kratɛr]
magma	магма (ж)	['maɦma]
lava	лава (ж)	['lawa]
molten (~ lava)	розжарений	[roz'ʒarɛnij]
canyon	каньйон (ч)	[kanʲ'jon]
gorge	ущелина (ж)	[u'ɕɛlina]

crevice	ущелина (c)	[uˈɕɛlina]
pass, col	перевал (ч)	[pɛrɛˈwal]
plateau	плато (c)	[ˈplato]
cliff	скеля (ж)	[ˈskɛlʲa]
hill	горб (ч)	[ɦorb]

glacier	льодовик (ч)	[lʲodoˈwik]
waterfall	водоспад (ч)	[wodosˈpad]
geyser	гейзер (ч)	[ˈɦɛjzɛr]
lake	озеро (c)	[ˈɔzɛro]

plain	рівнина (ж)	[riwˈnina]
landscape	краєвид (ч)	[kraɛˈwid]
echo	луна (ж)	[luˈna]

alpinist	альпініст (ч)	[alʲpiˈnist]
rock climber	скелелаз (ч)	[skɛlɛˈlaz]
to conquer (in climbing)	підкоряти	[pidkoˈrʲati]
climb (an easy ~)	підніманння (c)	[pidniˈmanʲa]

80. Mountains names

The Alps	Альпи (мн)	[ˈalʲpi]
Mont Blanc	Монблан (ч)	[monˈblan]
The Pyrenees	Піренеї (мн)	[pirɛˈnɛji]

The Carpathians	Карпати (мн)	[karˈpati]
The Ural Mountains	Уральські гори (мн)	[uˈralʲsʲki ˈɦori]
The Caucasus Mountains	Кавказ (ч)	[kawˈkaz]
Mount Elbrus	Ельбрус (ч)	[ɛlʲbˈrus]

The Altai Mountains	Алтай (ч)	[alˈtaj]
The Tian Shan	Тянь-Шань (мн)	[tʲanʲ ˈʃanʲ]
The Pamir Mountains	Памір (ч)	[paˈmir]
The Himalayas	Гімалаї (мн)	[ɦimaˈlaji]
Mount Everest	Еверест (ч)	[ɛwɛˈrɛst]

| The Andes | Анди (мн) | [ˈandi] |
| Mount Kilimanjaro | Кіліманджаро (ж) | [kilimanˈdʒaro] |

81. Rivers

river	ріка (ж)	[ˈrika]
spring (natural source)	джерело (c)	[dʒɛrɛˈlɔ]
riverbed (river channel)	річище (c)	[ˈritʃiɕɛ]
basin (river valley)	басейн (ч)	[baˈsɛjn]
to flow into …	упадати	[upaˈdati]
tributary	притока (ж)	[priˈtɔka]

bank (of river)	берег (ч)	['bɛrɛɦ]
current (stream)	течія (ж)	['tɛtʃiɐ]
downstream (adv)	вниз за течією (ж)	[wniz za 'tɛtʃiɛʲu]
upstream (adv)	уверх по течії	[u'wɛrh po 'tɛtʃiji]

inundation	повінь (ж)	['powinʲ]
flooding	повінь (ж)	['powinʲ]
to overflow (vi)	розливатися	[rozlʲi'watisʲa]
to flood (vt)	затоплювати	[za'toplʲuwati]

| shallow (shoal) | мілина (ж) | [mili'na] |
| rapids | поріг (ч) | [po'riɦ] |

dam	гребля (ж)	['ɦrɛblʲa]
canal	канал (ч)	[ka'nal]
reservoir (artificial lake)	водосховище (с)	[wodo'showiɕɛ]
sluice, lock	шлюз (ч)	[ʃlʲuz]

water body (pond, etc.)	водоймище (с)	[wo'dojmiɕɛ]
swamp (marshland)	болото (с)	[bo'loto]
bog, marsh	трясовина (ж)	[trʲasowi'na]
whirlpool	вир (ч)	[wir]

stream (brook)	струмок (ч)	[stru'mok]
drinking (ab. water)	питний	['pitnij]
fresh (~ water)	прісний	['prisnij]

| ice | крига (ж) | ['kriɦa] |
| to freeze over (ab. river, etc.) | замерзнути | [za'mɛrznuti] |

82. Rivers' names

| Seine | Сена (ж) | ['sɛna] |
| Loire | Луара (ж) | [lu'ara] |

Thames	Темза (ж)	['tɛmza]
Rhine	Рейн (ч)	[rɛjn]
Danube	Дунай (ч)	[du'naj]

Volga	Волга (ж)	['wolɦa]
Don	Дон (ч)	[don]
Lena	Лена (ж)	['lɛna]

Yellow River	Хуанхе (ж)	[huan'hɛ]
Yangtze	Янцзи (ж)	[jants'zi]
Mekong	Меконг (ч)	[mɛ'konɦ]
Ganges	Ганг (ч)	[ɦanɦ]
Nile River	Ніл (ч)	[nil]
Congo River	Конго (ж)	['konɦo]

Okavango River	Окаванго (ж)	[oka'wanɦo]
Zambezi River	Замбезі (ж)	[zam'bɛzi]
Limpopo River	Лімпопо (ж)	[limpo'pɔ]
Mississippi River	Міссісіпі (ж)	[misi'sipi]

83. Forest

| forest, wood | ліс (ч) | [lis] |
| forest (as adj) | лісовий | [liso'wij] |

thick forest	хаща (ж)	['haɕa]
grove	гай (ч)	[ɦaj]
forest clearing	галявина (ж)	[ɦa'lʲawina]

| thicket | хащі (мн) | ['haɕi] |
| scrubland | чагарник (ч) | [ʧa'ɦarnik] |

| footpath (troddenpath) | стежина (ж) | [stɛ'ʒina] |
| gully | яр (ч) | [jar] |

tree	дерево (с)	['dɛrɛwo]
leaf	листок (ч)	[lis'tɔk]
leaves (foliage)	листя (с)	['listʲa]

fall of leaves	листопад (ч)	[listo'pad]
to fall (ab. leaves)	опадати	[opa'dati]
top (of the tree)	верхівка (ж)	[wɛr'hiwka]

branch	гілка (ж)	['ɦilka]
bough	сук (ч)	[suk]
bud (on shrub, tree)	брунька (ж)	['brunʲka]
needle (of pine tree)	голка (ж)	['ɦɔlka]
pine cone	шишка (ж)	['ʃiʃka]

hollow (in a tree)	дупло (с)	[dup'lɔ]
nest	гніздо (с)	[ɦniz'dɔ]
burrow (animal hole)	нора (ж)	[no'ra]

trunk	стовбур (ч)	['stɔwbur]
root	корінь (ч)	['kɔrinʲ]
bark	кора (ж)	[ko'ra]
moss	мох (ч)	[moh]

to uproot (remove trees or tree stumps)	корчувати	[korʧu'wati]
to chop down	рубати	[ru'bati]
to deforest (vt)	вирубувати	[wi'rubuwati]
tree stump	пень (ч)	[pɛnʲ]
campfire	багаття (с)	[ba'ɦattʲa]
forest fire	пожежа (ж)	[po'ʒɛʒa]

to extinguish (v)	тушити	[tu'ʃiti]
forest ranger	лісник (ч)	[lis'nik]
protection	охорона (ж)	[oho'rɔna]
to protect (~ nature)	охороняти	[ohoro'nʲati]
poacher	браконьєр (ч)	[brako'nʲɛr]
steel trap	пастка (ж)	['pastka]

to gather, to pick (v)	збирати	[zbi'rati]
to lose one's way	заблукати	[zablu'kati]

84. Natural resources

natural resources	природні ресурси (мн)	[pri'rɔdni rɛ'sursi]
minerals	корисні копалини (мн)	['kɔrisni ko'palini]
deposits	поклади (мн)	['pɔkladi]
field (e.g., oilfield)	родовище (с)	[ro'dɔwiɕɛ]

to mine (extract)	добувати	[dobu'wati]
mining (extraction)	добування (с)	[dobu'wanʲa]
ore	руда (ж)	[ru'da]
mine (e.g., for coal)	копальня (ж)	[ko'palʲnʲa]
shaft (mine ~)	шахта (ж)	['ʃahta]
miner	шахтар (ч)	[ʃah'tar]

gas (natural ~)	газ (ч)	[ɦaz]
gas pipeline	газопровід (ч)	[ɦazopro'wid]

oil (petroleum)	нафта (ж)	['nafta]
oil pipeline	нафтопровід (ч)	[nafto'prɔwid]
oil well	нафтова вишка (ж)	['naftowa 'wiʃka]
derrick (tower)	свердлова вежа (ж)	[swɛrd'lɔwa 'wɛʒa]
tanker	танкер (ч)	['tankɛr]

sand	пісок (ч)	[pi'sɔk]
limestone	вапняк (ч)	[wap'nʲak]
gravel	гравій (ч)	['ɦrawij]
peat	торф (ч)	[torf]
clay	глина (ж)	['ɦlina]
coal	вугілля (с)	[wu'ɦilʲa]

iron (ore)	залізо (с)	[za'lizo]
gold	золото (с)	['zɔloto]
silver	срібло (с)	['sriblo]
nickel	нікель (ч)	['nikɛlʲ]
copper	мідь (ж)	[midʲ]

zinc	цинк (ч)	['tsink]
manganese	марганець (ч)	['marɦanɛts]
mercury	ртуть (ж)	[rtutʲ]
lead	свинець (ч)	[swi'nɛts]

mineral	мінерал (ч)	[minɛ'ral]
crystal	кристал (ч)	[kris'tal]
marble	мармур (ч)	['marmur]
uranium	уран (ч)	[u'ran]

85. Weather

weather	погода (ж)	[po'ɦɔda]
weather forecast	прогноз (ч) погоди (ж)	[proɦ'nɔz po'ɦɔdi]
temperature	температура (ж)	[tɛmpɛra'tura]
thermometer	термометр (ч)	[tɛr'mɔmɛtr]
barometer	барометр (ч)	[ba'rɔmɛtr]

humidity	вологість (ж)	[woloɦistʲ]
heat (extreme ~)	спека (ж)	['spɛka]
hot (torrid)	гарячий	[ɦa'rʲatʃij]
it's hot	спекотно	[spɛ'kɔtno]

| it's warm | тепло | ['tɛplo] |
| warm (moderately hot) | теплий | ['tɛplʲij] |

| it's cold | холодно | ['hɔlodno] |
| cold (adj) | холодний | [ho'lɔdnij] |

sun	сонце (с)	['sɔntsɛ]
to shine (vi)	світити	[swi'titi]
sunny (day)	сонячний	['sɔnʲatʃnij]
to come up (vi)	зійти	[zij'ti]
to set (vi)	сісти	['sisti]

cloud	хмара (ж)	['hmara]
cloudy (adj)	хмарний	['hmarnij]
rain cloud	хмара (ж)	['hmara]
somber (gloomy)	похмурний	[poh'murnij]

rain	дощ (ч)	[doɕ]
it's raining	йде дощ	[jdɛ doɕ]
rainy (~ day, weather)	дощовий	[doɕo'wij]
to drizzle (vi)	накрапати	[nakra'pati]

pouring rain	проливний дощ (ч)	[proliw'nij doɕ]
downpour	злива (ж)	['zliwa]
heavy (e.g., ~ rain)	сильний	['silʲnij]
puddle	калюжа (ж)	[ka'lʲuʒa]
to get wet (in rain)	мокнути	['mɔknuti]

fog (mist)	туман (ч)	[tu'man]
foggy	туманний	[tu'manij]
snow	сніг (ч)	[sniɦ]
it's snowing	йде сніг (ч)	[jdɛ sniɦ]

86. Severe weather. Natural disasters

thunderstorm	гроза (ж)	[ɦroˈza]
lightning (~ strike)	блискавка (ж)	[ˈblɪskawka]
to flash (vi)	блискати	[ˈblɪskatɪ]
thunder	грім (ч)	[ɦrim]
to thunder (vi)	гриміти	[ɦriˈmitɪ]
it's thundering	гримить грім	[ɦriˈmitʲ ɦrim]
hail	град (ч)	[ɦrad]
it's hailing	йде град	[jdɛ ɦrad]
to flood (vt)	затопити	[zatoˈpitɪ]
flood, inundation	повінь (ж)	[ˈpɔwinʲ]
earthquake	землетрус (ч)	[zɛmlɛtˈrus]
tremor, quake	поштовх (ч)	[ˈpɔʃtowh]
epicenter	епіцентр (ч)	[ɛpiˈʦɛntr]
eruption	виверження (с)	[ˈwiwɛrʒɛnʲa]
lava	лава (ж)	[ˈlawa]
twister	смерч (ч)	[smɛrʧ]
tornado	торнадо (ч)	[torˈnado]
typhoon	тайфун (ч)	[tajˈfun]
hurricane	ураган (ч)	[uraɦan]
storm	буря (ж)	[ˈburʲa]
tsunami	цунамі (с)	[ʦuˈnami]
cyclone	циклон (ч)	[ʦikˈlɔn]
bad weather	негода (ж)	[nɛˈɦɔda]
fire (accident)	пожежа (ж)	[poˈʒɛʒa]
disaster	катастрофа (ж)	[kataˈstrɔfa]
meteorite	метеорит (ч)	[mɛtɛoˈrit]
avalanche	лавина (ж)	[laˈwina]
snowslide	обвал (ч)	[obˈwal]
blizzard	заметіль (ж)	[zamɛˈtilʲ]
snowstorm	завірюха (ж)	[zawiˈrʲuha]

FAUNA

87. Mammals. Predators

predator	хижак (ч)	[hi'ʒak]
tiger	тигр (ч)	[tiɦr]
lion	лев (ч)	[lɛw]
wolf	вовк (ч)	[wowk]
fox	лисиця (ж)	[lɨ'sitsʲa]

jaguar	ягуар (ч)	[jaɦu'ar]
leopard	леопард (ч)	[lɛo'pard]
cheetah	гепард (ч)	[ɦɛ'pard]

black panther	пантера (ж)	[pan'tɛra]
puma	пума (ж)	['puma]
snow leopard	сніговий барс (ч)	[sniɦo'wɨj bars]
lynx	рись (ж)	[risʲ]

coyote	койот (ч)	[ko'jot]
jackal	шакал (ч)	[ʃa'kal]
hyena	гієна (ж)	[ɦi'ɛna]

88. Wild animals

animal	тварина (ж)	[twa'rɨna]
beast (animal)	звір (ч)	[zwir]

squirrel	білка (ж)	['bilka]
hedgehog	їжак (ч)	[ji'ʒak]
hare	заєць (ч)	['zaɛts]
rabbit	кріль (ч)	[krilʲ]

badger	борсук (ч)	[bor'suk]
raccoon	єнот (ч)	[ɛ'nɔt]
hamster	хом'як (ч)	[ho'mʲak]
marmot	бабак (ч)	[ba'bak]

mole	кріт (ч)	[krit]
mouse	миша (ж)	['mɨʃa]
rat	щур (ч)	[ɕur]
bat	кажан (ч)	[ka'ʒan]

ermine	горностай (ч)	[ɦorno'staj]
sable	соболь (ч)	['sɔbolʲ]
marten	куниця (ж)	[ku'nitsʲa]

weasel	ласка (ж)	['laska]
mink	норка (ж)	['nɔrka]
beaver	бобер (ч)	[bo'bɛr]
otter	видра (ж)	['wɨdra]
horse	кінь (ч)	[kinʲ]
moose	лось (ч)	[losʲ]
deer	олень (ч)	['ɔlɛnʲ]
camel	верблюд (ч)	[wɛr'blʲud]
bison	бізон (ч)	[bi'zɔn]
aurochs	зубр (ч)	[zubr]
buffalo	буйвіл (ч)	['bujwil]
zebra	зебра (ж)	['zɛbra]
antelope	антилопа (ж)	[anti'lɔpa]
roe deer	косуля (ж)	[ko'sulʲa]
fallow deer	лань (ж)	[lanʲ]
chamois	сарна (ж)	['sarna]
wild boar	вепр (ч)	[wɛpr]
whale	кит (ч)	[kit]
seal	тюлень (ч)	[tʲu'lɛnʲ]
walrus	морж (ч)	[mɔrʒ]
fur seal	котик (ч)	['kɔtik]
dolphin	дельфін (ч)	[dɛlʲ'fin]
bear	ведмідь (ч)	[wɛd'midʲ]
polar bear	білий ведмідь (ч)	['bilɨj wɛd'midʲ]
panda	панда (ж)	['panda]
monkey	мавпа (ж)	['mawpa]
chimpanzee	шимпанзе (ч)	[ʃimpan'zɛ]
orangutan	орангутанг (ч)	[oranɦu'tanɦ]
gorilla	горила (ж)	[ɦo'rila]
macaque	макака (ж)	[ma'kaka]
gibbon	гібон (ч)	[ɦi'bɔn]
elephant	слон (ч)	[slon]
rhinoceros	носоріг (ч)	[noso'riɦ]
giraffe	жирафа (ж)	[ʒirafa]
hippopotamus	бегемот (ч)	[bɛɦɛ'mɔt]
kangaroo	кенгуру (ч)	[kɛnɦu'ru]
koala (bear)	коала (ч)	[ko'ala]
mongoose	мангуст (ч)	[ma'nɦust]
chinchilla	шиншила (ж)	[ʃin'ʃila]
skunk	скунс (ч)	[skuns]
porcupine	дикобраз (ч)	[dɨko'braz]

89. Domestic animals

cat	кішка (ж)	['kiʃka]
tomcat	кіт (ч)	[kit]
horse	коняка (ж)	[ko'nʲaka]
stallion (male horse)	жеребець (ч)	[ʒɛrɛ'bɛʦ]
mare	кобила (ж)	[ko'bɨla]
cow	корова (ж)	[ko'rɔwa]
bull	бик (ч)	[bɨk]
ox	віл (ч)	[wil]
sheep (ewe)	вівця (ж)	[wiw'ʦʲa]
ram	баран (ч)	[ba'ran]
goat	коза (ж)	[ko'za]
billy goat, he-goat	козел (ч)	[ko'zɛl]
donkey	осел (ч)	[o'sɛl]
mule	мул (ч)	[mul]
pig, hog	свиня (ж)	[swɨ'nʲa]
piglet	порося (с)	[poro'sʲa]
rabbit	кріль (ч)	[krilʲ]
hen (chicken)	курка (ж)	['kurka]
rooster	півень (ч)	['piwɛnʲ]
duck	качка (ж)	['katʃka]
drake	качур (ч)	['katʃur]
goose	гусак (ч)	[ɦu'sak]
tom turkey, gobbler	індик (ч)	[in'dɨk]
turkey (hen)	індичка (ж)	[in'dɨtʃka]
domestic animals	домашні тварини (мн)	[do'maʃni twa'rɨni]
tame (e.g., ~ hamster)	ручний	[rutʃ'nɨj]
to tame (vt)	приручати	[priru'tʃati]
to breed (vt)	вирощувати	[wɨ'rɔɕuwati]
farm	ферма (ж)	['fɛrma]
poultry	свійські птахи (мн)	['swijsʲki pta'hi]
cattle	худоба (ж)	[ɦu'dɔba]
herd (cattle)	стадо (с)	['stado]
stable	конюшня (ж)	[ko'nʲuʃnʲa]
pigpen	свинарник (ч)	[swɨ'narnɨk]
cowshed	корівник (ч)	[ko'riwnɨk]
rabbit hutch	крільчатник (ч)	[krilʲ'tʃatnɨk]
hen house	курник (ч)	[kur'nɨk]

90. Birds

bird	птах (ч)	[ptah]
pigeon	голуб (ч)	['hɔlub]
sparrow	горобець (ч)	[hɔro'bɛts]
tit (great tit)	синиця (ж)	[si'nitsʲa]
magpie	сорока (ж)	[so'rɔka]

raven	ворон (ч)	['wɔron]
crow	ворона (ж)	[wo'rɔna]
jackdaw	галка (ж)	['halka]
rook	грак (ч)	[hrak]

duck	качка (ж)	['katʃka]
goose	гусак (ч)	[hu'sak]
pheasant	фазан (ч)	[fa'zan]

eagle	орел (ч)	[o'rɛl]
hawk	яструб (ч)	['ʲastrub]
falcon	сокіл (ч)	['sɔkil]
vulture	гриф (ч)	[hrif]
condor (Andean ~)	кондор (ч)	['kɔndor]

swan	лебідь (ч)	['lɛbidʲ]
crane	журавель (ч)	[ʒura'wɛlʲ]
stork	чорногуз (ч)	[tʃorno'huz]

parrot	папуга (ч)	[pa'puha]
hummingbird	колібрі (ч)	[ko'libri]
peacock	пава (ж)	['pawa]

ostrich	страус (ч)	['straus]
heron	чапля (ж)	['tʃaplʲa]
flamingo	фламінго (с)	[fla'minho]
pelican	пелікан (ч)	[pɛli'kan]

| nightingale | соловей (ч) | [solo'wɛj] |
| swallow | ластівка (ж) | ['lastiwka] |

thrush	дрізд (ч)	[drizd]
song thrush	співучий дрізд (ч)	[spi'wutʃij 'drizd]
blackbird	чорний дрізд (ч)	['tʃornij 'drizd]

swift	стриж (ч)	['striʒ]
lark	жайворонок (ч)	['ʒajworonok]
quail	перепел (ч)	['pɛrɛpɛl]

woodpecker	дятел (ч)	['dʲatɛl]
cuckoo	зозуля (ж)	[zo'zulʲa]
owl	сова (ж)	[so'wa]
eagle owl	пугач (ч)	[pu'hatʃ]

wood grouse	глухар (ч)	[ɦlu'har]
black grouse	тетерук (ч)	[tɛtɛ'ruk]
partridge	куріпка (ж)	[ku'ripka]

starling	шпак (ч)	[ʃpak]
canary	канарка (ж)	[ka'narka]
hazel grouse	рябчик (ч)	['rʲabtʃik]
chaffinch	зяблик (ч)	['zʲablik]
bullfinch	снігур (ч)	[sni'ɦur]

seagull	чайка (ж)	['tʃajka]
albatross	альбатрос (ч)	[alʲbat'rɔs]
penguin	пінгвін (ч)	[pinɦ'win]

91. Fish. Marine animals

bream	лящ (ч)	[lʲaɕ]
carp	короп (ч)	['kɔrop]
perch	окунь (ч)	['ɔkunʲ]
catfish	сом (ч)	[som]
pike	щука (ж)	['ɕuka]

| salmon | лосось (ч) | [lo'sɔsʲ] |
| sturgeon | осетер (ч) | [osɛ'tɛr] |

herring	оселедець (ч)	[osɛ'lɛdɛts]
Atlantic salmon	сьомга (ж)	['sʲomɦa]
mackerel	скумбрія (ж)	['skumbrʲia]
flatfish	камбала (ж)	[kamba'la]

zander, pike perch	судак (ч)	[su'dak]
cod	тріска (ж)	[tris'ka]
tuna	тунець (ч)	[tu'nɛts]
trout	форель (ж)	[fo'rɛlʲ]

eel	вугор (ч)	[wu'ɦɔr]
electric ray	електричний скат (ч)	[ɛlɛkt'ritʃnij skat]
moray eel	мурена (ж)	[mu'rɛna]
piranha	піранья (ж)	[pi'ranʲa]

shark	акула (ж)	[a'kula]
dolphin	дельфін (ч)	[dɛlʲ'fin]
whale	кит (ч)	[kit]

crab	краб (ч)	[krab]
jellyfish	медуза (ж)	[mɛ'duza]
octopus	восьминіг (ч)	[wosʲmi'niɦ]

| starfish | морська зірка (ж) | [morsʲ'ka 'zirka] |
| sea urchin | морський їжак (ч) | [morsʲ'kij ji'ʒak] |

seahorse	морський коник (ч)	[morsʲˈkij ˈkɔnɨk]
oyster	устриця (ж)	[ˈustrɨtsʲa]
shrimp	креветка (ж)	[krɛˈwɛtka]
lobster	омар (ч)	[oˈmar]
spiny lobster	лангуст (ч)	[lanˈɦust]

92. Amphibians. Reptiles

| snake | змія (ж) | [zmiˈʲa] |
| venomous (snake) | отруйний | [otˈrujnɨj] |

viper	гадюка (ж)	[ɦaˈdʲuka]
cobra	кобра (ж)	[ˈkɔbra]
python	пітон (ч)	[piˈtɔn]
boa	удав (ч)	[uˈdaw]

grass snake	вуж (ч)	[wuʒ]
rattle snake	гримуча змія (ж)	[ɦrɨˈmutʃa zmiˈʲa]
anaconda	анаконда (ж)	[anaˈkɔnda]

lizard	ящірка (ж)	[ˈʲaɕirka]
iguana	ігуана (ж)	[iɦuˈana]
monitor lizard	варан (ч)	[waˈran]
salamander	саламандра (ж)	[salaˈmandra]
chameleon	хамелеон (ч)	[ɦamɛlɛˈɔn]
scorpion	скорпіон (ч)	[skorpiˈɔn]

turtle	черепаха (ж)	[tʃɛrɛˈpaha]
frog	жабка (ж)	[ˈʒabka]
toad	жаба (ж)	[ˈʒaba]
crocodile	крокодил (ч)	[krokoˈdɨl]

93. Insects

insect, bug	комаха (ж)	[koˈmaha]
butterfly	метелик (ч)	[mɛˈtɛlɨk]
ant	мураха (ж)	[muˈraha]
fly	муха (ж)	[ˈmuha]
mosquito	комар (ч)	[koˈmar]
beetle	жук (ч)	[ʒuk]

wasp	оса (ж)	[oˈsa]
bee	бджола (ж)	[bdʐoˈla]
bumblebee	джміль (ч)	[dʐmilʲ]
gadfly (botfly)	овід (ч)	[ˈɔwid]

| spider | павук (ч) | [paˈwuk] |
| spiderweb | павутиння (с) | [pawuˈtɨnʲa] |

dragonfly	бабка (ж)	['babka]
grasshopper	коник (ч)	['kɔnik]
moth (night butterfly)	метелик (ч)	[mɛ'tɛlik]

cockroach	тарган (ч)	[tar'ɦan]
tick	кліщ (ч)	[kliɕ]
flea	блоха (ж)	['blɔha]
midge	мошка (ж)	['mɔʃka]

locust	сарана (ж)	[sara'na]
snail	равлик (ч)	['rawlik]
cricket	цвіркун (ч)	[ʦwir'kun]
lightning bug	світлячок (ч)	[switlʲa'ʧɔk]
ladybug	сонечко (с)	['sɔnɛʧko]
cockchafer	хрущ (ч)	[hruɕ]

leech	п'явка (ж)	['pʲawka]
caterpillar	гусениця (ж)	['husɛnitsʲa]
earthworm	черв'як (ч)	[ʧɛr'wʲak]
larva	личинка (ж)	[li'ʧinka]

FLORA

T&P Books Publishing

tree	дерево (с)	['dɛrɛwo]
deciduous (adj)	модринове	[mod'rinowɛ]
coniferous (adj)	хвойне	['hwɔjnɛ]
evergreen (adj)	вічнозелене	[witʃnozɛ'lɛnɛ]

apple tree	яблуня (ж)	['ʲablunʲa]
pear tree	груша (ж)	['ɦruʃa]
sweet cherry tree	черешня (ж)	[tʃɛ'rɛʃnʲa]
sour cherry tree	вишня (ж)	['wiʃnʲa]
plum tree	слива (ж)	['sɫiwa]

birch	береза (ж)	[bɛ'rɛza]
oak	дуб (ч)	[dub]
linden tree	липа (ж)	['ɫipa]
aspen	осика (ж)	[o'sɨka]
maple	клен (ч)	[klɛn]

spruce	ялина (ж)	[ja'ɫina]
pine	сосна (ж)	[sos'na]
larch	модрина (ж)	[mod'rina]

| fir tree | ялиця (ж) | [ja'ɫitsʲa] |
| cedar | кедр (ч) | [kɛdr] |

| poplar | тополя (ж) | [to'pɔlʲa] |
| rowan | горобина (ж) | [ɦoro'bina] |

| willow | верба (ж) | [wɛr'ba] |
| alder | вільха (ж) | ['wilʲha] |

| beech | бук (ч) | [buk] |
| elm | в'яз (ч) | [wʲʲaz] |

| ash (tree) | ясен (ч) | ['ʲasɛn] |
| chestnut | каштан (ч) | [kaʃtan] |

magnolia	магнолія (ж)	[maɦ'nɔliʲa]
palm tree	пальма (ж)	['palʲma]
cypress	кипарис (ч)	[kipa'ris]

mangrove	мангрове дерево (с)	['manɦrowɛ 'dɛrɛwo]
baobab	баобаб (ч)	[bao'bab]
eucalyptus	евкаліпт (ч)	[ɛwka'lipt]
sequoia	секвоя (ж)	[sɛk'wɔʲa]

95. Shrubs

bush	кущ (ч)	[kuɕ]
shrub	кущі (мн)	[ku'ɕi]
grapevine	виноград (ч)	[wino'ɦrad]
vineyard	виноградник (ч)	[wino'ɦradnik]
raspberry bush	малина (ж)	[ma'lina]
redcurrant bush	порічки (мн)	[po'ritʃki]
gooseberry bush	аґрус (ч)	['agrus]
acacia	акація (ж)	[a'katsiʲa]
barberry	барбарис (ч)	[barba'ris]
jasmine	жасмин (ч)	[ʒas'min]
juniper	ялівець (ч)	[jali'wɛts]
rosebush	трояндовий кущ (ч)	[tro'ʲandowij kuɕ]
dog rose	шипшина (ж)	[ʃip'ʃina]

96. Fruits. Berries

apple	яблуко (с)	['ʲabluko]
pear	груша (ж)	['ɦruʃa]
plum	слива (ж)	['sliwa]
strawberry (garden ~)	полуниця (ж)	[polu'nitsʲa]
sour cherry	вишня (ж)	['wiʃnʲa]
sweet cherry	черешня (ж)	[tʃɛ'rɛʃnʲa]
grape	виноград (ч)	[wino'ɦrad]
raspberry	малина (ж)	[ma'lina]
blackcurrant	чорна смородина (ж)	['tʃɔrna smo'rɔdina]
redcurrant	порічки (мн)	[po'ritʃki]
gooseberry	аґрус (ч)	['agrus]
cranberry	журавлина (ж)	[ʒuraw'lina]
orange	апельсин (ч)	[apɛlʲ'sin]
mandarin	мандарин (ч)	[manda'rin]
pineapple	ананас (ч)	[ana'nas]
banana	банан (ч)	[ba'nan]
date	фінік (ч)	['finik]
lemon	лимон (ч)	[li'mɔn]
apricot	абрикос (ч)	[abri'kɔs]
peach	персик (ч)	['pɛrsik]
kiwi	ківі (ч)	['kiwi]
grapefruit	грейпфрут (ч)	[ɦrɛjp'frut]
berry	ягода (ж)	['ʲaɦoda]

berries	ягоди (мн)	['jaɦodi]
cowberry	брусниця (ж)	[brus'nitsʲa]
wild strawberry	суниця (ж)	[su'nitsʲa]
bilberry	чорниця (ж)	[tʃor'nitsʲa]

97. Flowers. Plants

| flower | квітка (ж) | ['kwitka] |
| bouquet (of flowers) | букет (ч) | [bu'kɛt] |

rose (flower)	троянда (ж)	[tro'ʲanda]
tulip	тюльпан (ч)	[tʲulʲ'pan]
carnation	гвоздика (ж)	[ɦwoz'dika]
gladiolus	гладіолус (ч)	[ɦladi'ɔlus]

cornflower	волошка (ж)	[wo'lɔʃka]
harebell	дзвіночок (ч)	[dzwi'notʃok]
dandelion	кульбаба (ж)	[kulʲ'baba]
camomile	ромашка (ж)	[ro'maʃka]

aloe	алое (ч)	[a'lɔɛ]
cactus	кактус (ч)	['kaktus]
rubber plant, ficus	фікус (ч)	['fikus]

lily	лілея (ж)	[li'lɛʲa]
geranium	герань (ж)	[ɦɛ'ranʲ]
hyacinth	гіацинт (ч)	[ɦia'tsint]

mimosa	мімоза (ж)	[mi'mɔza]
narcissus	нарцис (ч)	[nar'tsis]
nasturtium	настурція (ж)	[nas'turtsiʲa]

orchid	орхідея (ж)	[orhi'dɛʲa]
peony	півонія (ж)	[pi'wɔniʲa]
violet	фіалка (ж)	[fi'alka]

pansy	братки (мн)	[brat'ki]
forget-me-not	незабудка (ж)	[nɛza'budka]
daisy	стокротки (мн)	[stok'rɔtki]

poppy	мак (ч)	[mak]
hemp	коноплі (мн)	[ko'nɔpli]
mint	м'ята (ж)	['mʲata]

| lily of the valley | конвалія (ж) | [kon'waliʲa] |
| snowdrop | пролісок (ч) | ['prɔlisok] |

nettle	кропива (ж)	[kropi'wa]
sorrel	щавель (ч)	[ɕa'wɛlʲ]
water lily	латаття (с)	[la'tattʲa]

fern	папороть (ж)	['paporotʲ]
lichen	лишайник (ч)	[liˈʃajnɨk]
greenhouse (tropical ~)	оранжерея (ж)	[oranʒɛˈrɛʲa]
lawn	газон (ч)	[ɦaˈzɔn]
flowerbed	клумба (ж)	[ˈklumba]
plant	рослина (ж)	[rosˈlina]
grass	трава (ж)	[traˈwa]
blade of grass	травинка (ж)	[traˈwinka]
leaf	листок (ч)	[lisˈtɔk]
petal	пелюстка (ж)	[pɛˈlʲustka]
stem	стебло (с)	[stɛbˈlɔ]
tuber	бульба (ж)	[ˈbulʲba]
young plant (shoot)	паросток (ч)	[ˈparostok]
thorn	колючка (ч)	[koˈlʲutʃka]
to blossom (vi)	цвісти	[tswisˈti]
to fade, to wither	в'янути	[ˈwʲanuti]
smell (odor)	запах (ч)	[ˈzapah]
to cut (flowers)	зрізати	[ˈzrizati]
to pick (a flower)	зірвати	[zirˈwati]

98. Cereals, grains

grain	зерно (с)	[zɛrˈnɔ]
cereal crops	зернові рослини (мн)	[zɛrnoˈwi rosˈlini]
ear (of barley, etc.)	колос (ч)	[ˈkɔlos]
wheat	пшениця (ж)	[pʃɛˈnitsʲa]
rye	жито (с)	[ˈʒito]
oats	овес (ч)	[oˈwɛs]
millet	просо (с)	[ˈprɔso]
barley	ячмінь (ч)	[jatʃˈminʲ]
corn	кукурудза (ж)	[kukuˈrudza]
rice	рис (ч)	[ris]
buckwheat	гречка (ж)	[ˈɦrɛtʃka]
pea plant	горох (ч)	[ɦoˈrɔh]
kidney bean	квасоля (ж)	[kwaˈsɔlʲa]
soy	соя (ж)	[ˈsɔʲa]
lentil	сочевиця (ж)	[sotʃɛˈwitsʲa]
beans (pulse crops)	боби (мн)	[boˈbɨ]

COUNTRIES OF
THE WORLD

T&P Books Publishing

Afghanistan	**Афганістан** (ч)	[afhani'stan]
Albania	**Албанія** (ж)	[al'baniᴵa]
Argentina	**Аргентина** (ж)	[arhɛn'tina]
Armenia	**Вірменія** (ж)	[wir'mɛniᴵa]
Australia	**Австралія** (ж)	[aw'straliᴵa]
Austria	**Австрія** (ж)	['awstriᴵa]
Azerbaijan	**Азербайджан** (ч)	[azɛrbaj'dʒan]

The Bahamas	**Багамські острови** (мн)	[ba'hamsᴵki ostro'wi]
Bangladesh	**Бангладеш** (ч)	[banhla'dɛʃ]
Belarus	**Білорусь** (ж)	[bilo'rusᴵ]
Belgium	**Бельгія** (ж)	['bɛlᴵhiᴵa]
Bolivia	**Болівія** (ж)	[bo'liwiᴵa]
Bosnia and Herzegovina	**Боснія** (ж) **і Герцеговина** (ж)	['bɔsniᴵa i hɛrtsɛho'wina]
Brazil	**Бразилія** (ж)	[bra'ziliᴵa]
Bulgaria	**Болгарія** (ж)	[bol'hariᴵa]

Cambodia	**Камбоджа** (ж)	[kam'bɔdʒa]
Canada	**Канада** (ж)	[ka'nada]
Chile	**Чилі** (ж)	['tʃili]
China	**Китай** (ч)	[ki'taj]
Colombia	**Колумбія** (ж)	[ko'lumbiᴵa]
Croatia	**Хорватія** (ж)	[hor'watiᴵa]
Cuba	**Куба** (ж)	['kuba]
Cyprus	**Кіпр** (ж)	[kipr]
Czech Republic	**Чехія** (ж)	['tʃɛhiᴵa]

Denmark	**Данія** (ж)	['daniᴵa]
Dominican Republic	**Домініканська республіка** (ж)	[domini'kansᴵka rɛs'publika]
Ecuador	**Еквадор** (ч)	[ɛkwa'dɔr]
Egypt	**Єгипет** (ч)	[ɛ'hipɛt]
England	**Англія** (ж)	['anhliᴵa]
Estonia	**Естонія** (ж)	[ɛs'toniᴵa]
Finland	**Фінляндія** (ж)	[fin'lᴵandiᴵa]
France	**Франція** (ж)	['frantsiᴵa]
French Polynesia	**Французька Полінезія** (ж)	[fran'tsuzᴵka poli'nɛziᴵa]

Georgia	**Грузія** (ж)	['hruziᴵa]
Germany	**Німеччина** (ж)	[ni'mɛtʃina]
Ghana	**Гана** (ж)	['hana]
Great Britain	**Великобританія** (ж)	[wɛlikobri'taniᴵa]
Greece	**Греція** (ж)	['hrɛtsiᴵa]

| Haiti | Гаїті (ч) | [ha'jiti] |
| Hungary | Угорщина (ж) | [u'horɡina] |

100. Countries. Part 2

Iceland	Ісландія (ж)	[is'landiʲa]
India	Індія (ж)	['indiʲa]
Indonesia	Індонезія (ж)	[indo'nɛziʲa]
Iran	Іран (ч)	[i'ran]
Iraq	Ірак (ч)	[i'rak]
Ireland	Ірландія (ж)	[ir'landiʲa]
Israel	Ізраїль (ч)	[iz'rajilʲ]
Italy	Італія (ж)	[i'taliʲa]

Jamaica	Ямайка (ж)	[ja'majka]
Japan	Японія (ж)	[ja'poniʲa]
Jordan	Йорданія (ж)	[ʲor'daniʲa]
Kazakhstan	Казахстан (ч)	[kazah'stan]
Kenya	Кенія (ж)	['kɛniʲa]
Kirghizia	Киргизстан (ч)	[kirhiz'stan]
Kuwait	Кувейт (ч)	[ku'wɛjt]

Laos	Лаос (ч)	[la'ɔs]
Latvia	Латвія (ж)	['latwiʲa]
Lebanon	Ліван (ч)	[li'wan]
Libya	Лівія (ж)	['liwiʲa]
Liechtenstein	Ліхтенштейн (ч)	[lihtɛn'ʃtɛjn]
Lithuania	Литва (ж)	[lit'wa]
Luxembourg	Люксембург (ч)	[lʲuksɛm'burɦ]

Macedonia (Republic of ~)	Македонія (ж)	[makɛ'dɔniʲa]
Madagascar	Мадагаскар (ч)	[madaɦa'skar]
Malaysia	Малайзія (ж)	[ma'lajziʲa]
Malta	Мальта (ж)	['malʲta]
Mexico	Мексика (ж)	['mɛksika]
Moldova, Moldavia	Молдова (ж)	[mol'dɔwa]

Monaco	Монако (с)	[mo'nako]
Mongolia	Монголія (ж)	[mon'ɦɔliʲa]
Montenegro	Чорногорія (ж)	[ʧorno'ɦɔriʲa]

| Morocco | Марокко (с) | [ma'rɔkko] |
| Myanmar | М'янма (ж) | ['mʲʲanma] |

Namibia	Намібія (ж)	[na'mibiʲa]
Nepal	Непал (ч)	[nɛ'pal]
Netherlands	Нідерланди (ж)	[nidɛr'landi]
New Zealand	Нова Зеландія (ж)	[no'wa zɛ'landiʲa]
North Korea	Північна Корея (ж)	[piw'niʧna ko'rɛʲa]
Norway	Норвегія (ж)	[nor'wɛɦiʲa]

101. Countries. Part 3

Pakistan	Пакистан (ч)	[paki'stan]
Palestine	Палестинська автономія (ж)	[palɛ'stins⁞ka awto'nɔmi⁞a]
Panama	Панама (ж)	[pa'nama]
Paraguay	Парагвай (ч)	[parah'waj]
Peru	Перу (ж)	[pɛ'ru]
Poland	Польща (ж)	['pɔl⁞ɕa]
Portugal	Португалія (ж)	[portu'hali⁞a]
Romania	Румунія (ж)	[ru'muni⁞a]
Russia	Росія (ж)	[ro'si⁞a]
Saudi Arabia	Саудівська Аравія (ж)	[sa'udiws⁞ka a'rawi⁞a]
Scotland	Шотландія (ж)	[ʃot'landi⁞a]
Senegal	Сенегал (ч)	[sɛnɛ'hal]
Serbia	Сербія (ж)	['sɛrbi⁞a]
Slovakia	Словаччина (ж)	[slo'watʃina]
Slovenia	Словенія (ж)	[slo'wɛni⁞a]
South Africa	Південно-Африканська Республіка (ж)	[piw'dɛno afri'kans⁞ka rɛs'publika]
South Korea	Південна Корея (ж)	[piw'dɛna ko'rɛ⁞a]
Spain	Іспанія (ж)	[ispani⁞a]
Suriname	Суринам (ч)	[suri'nam]
Sweden	Швеція (ж)	['ʃwɛtsi⁞a]
Switzerland	Швейцарія (ж)	[ʃwɛj'tsari⁞a]
Syria	Сирія (ж)	['siri⁞a]
Taiwan	Тайвань (ч)	[taj'wan⁞]
Tajikistan	Таджикистан (ч)	[tadʒiki'stan]
Tanzania	Танзанія (ж)	[tan'zani⁞a]
Tasmania	Тасманія (ж)	[tas'mani⁞a]
Thailand	Таїланд (ч)	[taji'land]
Tunisia	Туніс (ч)	[tu'nis]
Turkey	Туреччина (ж)	[tu'rɛtʃina]
Turkmenistan	Туркменістан (ч)	[turkmɛni'stan]
Ukraine	Україна (ж)	[ukra'jina]
United Arab Emirates	Об'єднані Арабські емірати	[o'b'ɛdnani a'rabs⁞ki ɛmi'rati]
United States of America	Сполучені Штати Америки	[spo'lutʃɛni 'ʃtati a'mɛriki]
Uruguay	Уругвай (ч)	[uruh'waj]
Uzbekistan	Узбекистан (ч)	[uzbɛki'stan]
Vatican	Ватикан (ч)	[wati'kan]
Venezuela	Венесуела (ж)	[wɛnɛsu'ɛla]
Vietnam	В'єтнам (ч)	[w'ɛt'nam]
Zanzibar	Занзібар (ч)	[zanzi'bar]

GASTRONOMIC GLOSSARY

This section contains a lot of words and terms associated with food. This dictionary will make it easier for you to understand the menu at a restaurant and choose the right dish

T&P Books Publishing

English-Ukrainian gastronomic glossary

aftertaste	присмак (ч)	['prismak]
almond	мигдаль (ч)	[miɦ'dalʲ]
anise	аніс (ч)	['anis]
aperitif	аперитив (ч)	[apɛri'tiw]
appetite	апетит (ч)	[apɛ'tit]
appetizer	закуска (ж)	[za'kuska]
apple	яблуко (с)	['ʲabluko]
apricot	абрикос (ч)	[abri'kɔs]
artichoke	артишок (ч)	[arti'ʃɔk]
asparagus	спаржа (ж)	['sparʒa]
Atlantic salmon	сьомга (ж)	['sʲomɦa]
avocado	авокадо (с)	[awo'kado]
bacon	бекон (ч)	[bɛ'kɔn]
banana	банан (ч)	[ba'nan]
barley	ячмінь (ч)	[jatʃ'minʲ]
bartender	бармен (ч)	[bar'mɛn]
basil	базилік (ч)	[bazi'lik]
bay leaf	лавровий лист (ч)	[law'rɔwij list]
beans	боби (мн)	[bo'bɨ]
beef	яловичина (ж)	['ʲalowitʃina]
beer	пиво (с)	['piwo]
beetroot	буряк (ч)	[bu'rʲak]
bell pepper	перець (ч)	['pɛrɛts]
berries	ягоди (мн)	['ʲaɦodi]
berry	ягода (ж)	['ʲaɦoda]
bilberry	чорниця (ж)	[tʃor'nitsʲa]
birch bolete	підберезник (ч)	[pidbɛ'rɛznik]
bitter	гіркий	[ɦir'kij]
black coffee	чорна кава (ж)	['tʃɔrna 'kawa]
black pepper	чорний перець (ч)	['tʃɔrnij 'pɛrɛts]
black tea	чорний чай (ч)	['tʃɔrnij tʃaj]
blackberry	ожина (ж)	[o'ʒina]
blackcurrant	чорна смородина (ж)	['tʃɔrna smo'rɔdina]
boiled	варений	[wa'rɛnij]
bottle opener	відкривачка (ж)	[widkri'watʃka]
bread	хліб (ч)	[hlib]
breakfast	сніданок (ч)	[sni'danok]
bream	лящ (ч)	[lʲaɕ]
broccoli	капуста броколі (ж)	[ka'pusta 'brɔkoli]
Brussels sprouts	брюссельська капуста (ж)	[brʲu'sɛlʲsʲka ka'pusta]
buckwheat	гречка (ж)	['ɦrɛtʃka]
butter	вершкове масло (с)	[wɛrʃ'kɔwɛ 'maslo]
buttercream	крем (ч)	[krɛm]

cabbage	капуста (ж)	[ka'pusta]
cake	тістечко (с)	['tistɛtʃko]
cake	торт (ч)	[tort]
calorie	калорія (ж)	[ka'lɔriʲa]
can opener	відкривачка (ж)	[widkri'watʃka]
candy	цукерка (ж)	[ʦu'kɛrka]
canned food	консерви (мн)	[kon'sɛrwi]
cappuccino	кава (ж) з вершками	['kawa z wɛrʃ'kami]
caraway	кмин (ч)	[kmin]
carbohydrates	вуглеводи (ч)	[wuɦlɛ'wɔdi]
carbonated	газований	[ɦa'zɔwanij]
carp	короп (ч)	['kɔrop]
carrot	морква (ж)	['mɔrkwa]
catfish	сом (ч)	[som]
cauliflower	кольорова капуста (ж)	[kolʲo'rɔwa ka'pusta]
caviar	ікра (ж)	[ik'ra]
celery	селера (ж)	[sɛ'lɛra]
cep	білий гриб (ч)	['bilij 'ɦrib]
cereal crops	зернові рослини (мн)	[zɛrno'wi ros'lini]
cereal grains	крупа (ж)	[kru'pa]
champagne	шампанське (с)	[ʃam'pansʲkɛ]
chanterelle	лисичка (ж)	[liʲsitʃka]
check	рахунок (ч)	[ra'hunok]
cheese	сир (ч)	[sir]
chewing gum	жувальна гумка (ж)	[ʒu'walʲna 'ɦumka]
chicken	курка (ж)	['kurka]
chocolate	шоколад (ч)	[ʃoko'lad]
chocolate	шоколадний	[ʃoko'ladnij]
cinnamon	кориця (ж)	[ko'riʦʲa]
clear soup	бульйон (ч)	[bulʲon]
cloves	гвоздика (ж)	[ɦwoz'dika]
cocktail	коктейль (ч)	[kok'tɛjlʲ]
coconut	горіх (ч) кокосовий	[ɦo'rih ko'kɔsowij]
cod	тріска (ж)	[tris'ka]
coffee	кава (ж)	['kawa]
coffee with milk	кава (ж) з молоком	['kawa z molo'kɔm]
cognac	коньяк (ч)	[ko'nʲak]
cold	холодний	[ho'lɔdnij]
condensed milk	згущене молоко (с)	['zɦuɕɛnɛ molo'kɔ]
condiment	приправа (ж)	[prip'rawa]
confectionery	кондитерські вироби (мн)	[kon'ditɛrsʲki 'wirobi]
cookies	печиво (с)	['pɛtʃiwo]
coriander	коріандр (ч)	[kori'andr]
corkscrew	штопор (ч)	['ʃtɔpor]
corn	кукурудза (ж)	[kuku'ruʣa]
corn	кукурудза (ж)	[kuku'ruʣa]
cornflakes	кукурудзяні пластівці (мн)	[kuku'ruʣʲani plastiw'ʦi]
course, dish	страва (ж)	['strawa]
cowberry	брусниця (ж)	[brus'niʦʲa]
crab	краб (ч)	[krab]

cranberry	журавлина (ж)	[ʒuraw'lina]
cream	вершки (мн)	[wɛrʃ'ki]
crumb	крихта (ж)	['krihta]
cucumber	огірок (ч)	[ohi'rɔk]
cuisine	кухня (ж)	['kuhnʲa]
cup	чашка (ж)	['tʃaʃka]
dark beer	темне пиво (с)	['tɛmnɛ 'piwo]
date	фінік (ч)	['finik]
death cap	поганка (ж)	[po'hanka]
dessert	десерт (ч)	[dɛ'sɛrt]
diet	дієта (ж)	[di'ɛta]
dill	кріп (ч)	[krip]
dinner	вечеря (ж)	[wɛ'tʃɛrʲa]
dried	сушений	['suʃenij]
drinking water	питна вода (ж)	[pit'na wo'da]
duck	качка (ж)	['katʃka]
ear	колос (ч)	['kɔlos]
edible mushroom	їстівний гриб (ч)	[jis'tiwnij ɦrib]
eel	вугор (ч)	[wu'ɦɔr]
egg	яйце (с)	[jaj'tsɛ]
egg white	білок (ч)	[bi'lɔk]
egg yolk	жовток (ч)	[ʒow'tɔk]
eggplant	баклажан (ч)	[bakla'ʒan]
eggs	яйця (мн)	['ajtsʲa]
Enjoy your meal!	Смачного!	[smatʃ'nɔho]
fats	жири (мн)	[ʒi'ri]
fig	інжир (ч)	[in'ʒir]
filling	начинка (ж)	[na'tʃinka]
fish	риба (ж)	['riba]
flatfish	камбала (ж)	[kamba'la]
flour	борошно (с)	['bɔroʃno]
fly agaric	мухомор (ч)	[muho'mɔr]
food	їжа (ж)	['jiʒa]
fork	виделка (ж)	[wi'dɛlka]
freshly squeezed juice	свіжовижатий сік (ч)	[swiʒo'wiʒatij sik]
fried	смажений	['smaʒenij]
fried eggs	яєчня (ж)	[ja'ɛʃnʲa]
frozen	заморожений	[zamo'rɔʒenij]
fruit	фрукт (ч)	[frukt]
game	дичина (ж)	[ditʃi'na]
gammon	окіст (ч)	['ɔkist]
garlic	часник (ч)	[tʃas'nik]
gin	джин (ч)	[dʒin]
ginger	імбир (ч)	[im'bir]
glass	склянка (ж)	['sklʲanka]
glass	келих (ч)	['kɛlih]
goose	гусак (ч)	[ɦu'sak]
gooseberry	аґрус (ч)	['agrus]
grain	зерно (с)	[zɛr'nɔ]
grape	виноград (ч)	[wino'ɦrad]
grapefruit	грейпфрут (ч)	[ɦrɛjp'frut]
green tea	зелений чай (ч)	[zɛ'lɛnij tʃaj]

greens	зелень (ж)	['zɛlɛnʲ]
halibut	палтус (ч)	['paltus]
ham	шинка (ж)	['ʃinka]
hamburger	фарш (ч)	[farʃ]
hamburger	гамбургер (ч)	['hamburhɛr]
hazelnut	ліщина (ж)	[li'ɕina]
herring	оселедець (ч)	[osɛ'lɛdɛts]
honey	мед (ч)	[mɛd]
horseradish	хрін (ч)	[hrin]
hot	гарячий	[ha'rʲatʃij]
ice	лід (ч)	[lid]
ice-cream	морозиво (с)	[mo'rɔziwo]
instant coffee	розчинна кава (ж)	[roz'tʃina 'kawa]
jam	джем (ч)	[dʒɛm]
jam	варення (с)	[wa'rɛnʲa]
juice	сік (ч)	[sik]
kidney bean	квасоля (ж)	[kwa'sɔlʲa]
kiwi	ківі (ч)	['kiwi]
knife	ніж (ч)	[niʒ]
lamb	баранина (ж)	[ba'ranina]
lemon	лимон (ч)	[lɨ'mɔn]
lemonade	лимонад (ч)	[lɨmo'nad]
lentil	сочевиця (ж)	[sotʃɛ'witsʲa]
lettuce	салат (ч)	[sa'lat]
light beer	світле пиво (с)	['switlɛ 'piwo]
liqueur	лікер (ч)	[li'kɛr]
liquors	алкогольні напої (мн)	[alko'hɔlʲni na'pɔji]
liver	печінка (ж)	[pɛ'tʃinka]
lunch	обід (ч)	[o'bid]
mackerel	скумбрія (ж)	['skumbriʲa]
mandarin	мандарин (ч)	[manda'rin]
mango	манго (с)	['manho]
margarine	маргарин (ч)	[marha'rin]
marmalade	мармелад (ч)	[marmɛ'lad]
mashed potatoes	картопляне пюре (с)	[kartop'lʲanɛ pʲu'rɛ]
mayonnaise	майонез (ч)	[maʲo'nɛz]
meat	м'ясо (с)	['mʲʲaso]
melon	диня (ж)	['dinʲa]
menu	меню (с)	[mɛ'nʲu]
milk	молоко (с)	[molo'kɔ]
milkshake	молочний коктейль (ч)	[mo'lɔtʃnij kok'tɛjlʲ]
millet	просо (с)	['prɔso]
mineral water	мінеральна вода (ж)	[minɛ'ralʲna wo'da]
morel	зморшок (ч)	['zmɔrʃok]
mushroom	гриб (ч)	[hrib]
mustard	гірчиця (ж)	[hir'tʃitsʲa]
non-alcoholic	безалкогольний	[bɛzalko'hɔlʲnij]
noodles	локшина (ж)	[lokʃi'na]
oats	овес (ч)	[o'wɛs]
olive oil	олія (ж) оливкова	[o'liʲa o'liwkowa]
olives	оливки (мн)	[o'liwki]
omelet	омлет (ч)	[om'lɛt]

onion	цибуля (ж)	[tsi'bulʲa]
orange	апельсин (ч)	[apɛlʲ'sin]
orange juice	апельсиновий сік (ч)	[apɛlʲ'sinowij sik]
orange-cap boletus	підосичник (ч)	[pido'sitʃnik]
oyster	устриця (ж)	['ustritsʲa]
pâté	паштет (ч)	[paʃ'tɛt]
papaya	папайя (ж)	[pa'paʲa]
paprika	паприка (ж)	['paprika]
parsley	петрушка (ж)	[pɛt'ruʃka]
pasta	макарони (мн)	[maka'rɔni]
pea	горох (ч)	[ho'rɔh]
peach	персик (ч)	['pɛrsik]
peanut	арахіс (ч)	[a'rahis]
pear	груша (ж)	['hruʃa]
peel	шкірка (ж)	['ʃkirka]
perch	окунь (ч)	['ɔkunʲ]
pickled	маринований	[mari'nɔwanij]
pie	пиріг (ч)	[pi'rih]
piece	шматок (ч)	[ʃma'tɔk]
pike	щука (ж)	['ɕuka]
pike perch	судак (ч)	[su'dak]
pineapple	ананас (ч)	[ana'nas]
pistachios	фісташки (мн)	[fis'taʃki]
pizza	піца (ж)	['pitsa]
plate	тарілка (ж)	[ta'rilka]
plum	слива (ж)	['sliwa]
poisonous mushroom	отруйний гриб (ч)	[ot'rujnij hrib]
pomegranate	гранат (ч)	[hra'nat]
pork	свинина (ж)	[swi'nina]
porridge	каша (ж)	['kaʃa]
portion	порція (ж)	['portsiʲa]
potato	картопля (ж)	[kar'tɔplʲa]
proteins	білки (мн)	[bil'ki]
pub, bar	бар (ч)	[bar]
pumpkin	гарбуз (ч)	[har'buz]
rabbit	кріль (ч)	[krilʲ]
radish	редька (ж)	['rɛdʲka]
raisin	родзинки (мн)	[ro'dzinki]
raspberry	малина (ж)	[ma'lina]
recipe	рецепт (ч)	[rɛ'tsɛpt]
red pepper	червоний перець (ч)	[tʃɛr'wɔnij 'pɛrɛts]
red wine	червоне вино (с)	[tʃɛr'wɔnɛ wi'nɔ]
redcurrant	порічки (мн)	[po'ritʃki]
refreshing drink	прохолодній напій (ч)	[proho'lɔdnij na'pij]
rice	рис (ч)	[ris]
rum	ром (ч)	[rom]
russula	сироїжка (ж)	[siro'jiʒka]
rye	жито (с)	['ʒito]
saffron	шафран (ч)	[ʃaf'ran]
salad	салат (ч)	[sa'lat]
salmon	лосось (ч)	[lo'sɔsʲ]
salt	сіль (ж)	[silʲ]

salty	солоний	[so'lɔnij]
sandwich	канапка (ж)	[ka'napka]
sardine	сардина (ж)	[sar'dina]
sauce	соус (ч)	['sɔus]
saucer	блюдце (с)	['blʲudtsɛ]
sausage	ковбаса (ж)	[kowba'sa]
seafood	морепродукти (мн)	[morɛpro'dukti]
sesame	кунжут (ч)	[kun'ʒut]
shark	акула (ж)	[a'kula]
shrimp	креветка (ж)	[krɛ'wɛtka]
side dish	гарнір (ч)	[ɦar'nir]
slice	скибка (ж)	['skibka]
smoked	копчений	[kop'tʃɛnij]
soft drink	безалкогольний напій (ч)	[bɛzalko'ɦɔlʲnij na'pij]
soup	юшка (ж)	['ʲuʃka]
soup spoon	столова ложка (ж)	[sto'lɔwa 'lɔʒka]
sour cherry	вишня (ж)	['wiʃnʲa]
sour cream	сметана (ж)	[smɛ'tana]
soy	соя (ж)	['sɔʲa]
spaghetti	спагеті (мн)	[spa'ɦɛti]
sparkling	з газом	[z 'ɦazom]
spice	прянощі (мн)	[prʲa'nɔɕi]
spinach	шпинат (ч)	[ʃpi'nat]
spiny lobster	лангуст (ч)	[lan'ɦust]
spoon	ложка (ж)	['lɔʒka]
squid	кальмар (ч)	[kalʲ'mar]
steak	біфштекс (ч)	[bifʲʃtɛks]
still	без газу	[bɛz 'ɦazu]
strawberry	полуниця (ж)	[polu'nitsʲa]
sturgeon	осетрина (ж)	[osɛt'rina]
sugar	цукор (ч)	['tsukor]
sunflower oil	соняшникова олія (ж)	['sonʲaʃnikowa o'liʲa]
sweet	солодкий	[so'lɔdkij]
sweet cherry	черешня (ж)	[tʃɛ'rɛʃnʲa]
taste, flavor	смак (ч)	[smak]
tasty	смачний	[smatʃʲnij]
tea	чай (ч)	[tʃaj]
teaspoon	чайна ложка (ж)	['tʃajna 'lɔʒka]
tip	чайові (мн)	[tʃaʲo'wi]
tomato	помідор (ч)	[pomi'dɔr]
tomato juice	томатний сік (ч)	[to'matnij 'sik]
tongue	язик (ч)	[ja'zik]
toothpick	зубочистка (ж)	[zubo'tʃistka]
trout	форель (ж)	[fo'rɛlʲ]
tuna	тунець (ч)	[tu'nɛts]
turkey	індичка (ж)	[in'ditʃka]
turnip	ріпа (ж)	['ripa]
veal	телятина (ж)	[tɛ'lʲatina]
vegetable oil	олія (ж) рослинна	[o'liʲa ros'lina]
vegetables	овочі (мн)	['ɔwotʃi]
vegetarian	вегетаріанець (ч)	[wɛɦɛtari'anɛts]

vegetarian	вегетаріанський	[wɛhɛtari'ansʲkij]
vermouth	вермут (ч)	['wɛrmut]
vienna sausage	сосиска (ж)	[so'sɨska]
vinegar	оцет (ч)	['ɔtsɛt]
vitamin	вітамін (ч)	[wita'min]
vodka	горілка (ж)	[ɦo'rilka]
waffles	вафлі (мн)	['wafli]
waiter	офіціант (ч)	[ofitsi'ant]
waitress	офіціантка (ж)	[ofitsi'antka]
walnut	горіх (ч) волоський	[ɦo'rih wo'lɔsʲkij]
water	вода (ж)	[wo'da]
watermelon	кавун (ч)	[ka'wun]
wheat	пшениця (ж)	[pʃɛ'nɨtsʲa]
whiskey	віскі (с)	['wiski]
white wine	біле вино (с)	['bilɛ wɨ'nɔ]
wild strawberry	суниця (ж)	[su'nɨtsʲa]
wine	вино (с)	[wɨ'nɔ]
wine list	карта (ж) вин	['karta wɨn]
with ice	з льодом	[z lʲodom]
yogurt	йогурт (ч)	['jɔɦurt]
zucchini	кабачок (ч)	[kaba'tʃɔk]

Ukrainian-English gastronomic glossary

Ukrainian	Transcription	English
абрикос (ч)	[abri'kɔs]	apricot
авокадо (с)	[awo'kado]	avocado
аґрус (ч)	['agrus]	gooseberry
акула (ж)	[a'kula]	shark
алкогольні напої (мн)	[alko'hɔlʲni na'pɔjɨ]	liquors
ананас (ч)	[ana'nas]	pineapple
аніс (ч)	['anis]	anise
апельсин (ч)	[apɛlʲ'sɨn]	orange
апельсиновий сік (ч)	[apɛlʲ'sɨnowɨj sik]	orange juice
аперитив (ч)	[apɛri'tʲiw]	aperitif
апетит (ч)	[apɛ'tʲit]	appetite
арахіс (ч)	[a'rahis]	peanut
артишок (ч)	[arti'ʃɔk]	artichoke
базилік (ч)	[bazi'lik]	basil
баклажан (ч)	[bakla'ʒan]	eggplant
банан (ч)	[ba'nan]	banana
бар (ч)	[bar]	pub, bar
баранина (ж)	[ba'ranɨna]	lamb
бармен (ч)	[bar'mɛn]	bartender
без газу	[bɛz 'hazu]	still
безалкогольний	[bɛzalko'hɔlʲnɨj]	non-alcoholic
безалкогольний напій (ч)	[bɛzalko'hɔlʲnɨj na'pij]	soft drink
бекон (ч)	[bɛ'kɔn]	bacon
біле вино (с)	['bilɛ wɨ'nɔ]	white wine
білий гриб (ч)	['bilɨj 'hrib]	cep
білки (мн)	[bil'kɨ]	proteins
білок (ч)	[bi'lɔk]	egg white
біфштекс (ч)	[bif'ʃtɛks]	steak
блюдце (с)	['blʲudtsɛ]	saucer
боби (мн)	[bo'bɨ]	beans
борошно (с)	['bɔroʃno]	flour
брусниця (ж)	[brus'nʲitsʲa]	cowberry
брюссельська капуста (ж)	[brʲu'sɛlʲsʲka ka'pusta]	Brussels sprouts
бульйон (ч)	[bulʲon]	clear soup
буряк (ч)	[bu'rʲak]	beetroot
варений	[wa'rɛnɨj]	boiled
варення (с)	[wa'rɛnʲa]	jam
вафлі (мн)	['wafli]	waffles
вегетаріанець (ч)	[wɛɦɛtari'anɛts]	vegetarian
вегетаріанський	[wɛɦɛtari'ansʲkij]	vegetarian
вермут (ч)	['wɛrmut]	vermouth
вершки (мн)	[wɛrʃ'kɨ]	cream

вершкове масло (с)	[wɛrʃ'kɔwɛ 'maslo]	butter
вечеря (ж)	[wɛ'tʃɛrʲa]	dinner
виделка (ж)	[wi'dɛlka]	fork
вино (с)	[wi'nɔ]	wine
виноград (ч)	[wino'ɦrad]	grape
вишня (ж)	['wiʃnʲa]	sour cherry
відкривачка (ж)	[widkri'watʃka]	bottle opener
відкривачка (ж)	[widkri'watʃka]	can opener
віскі (с)	['wiski]	whiskey
вітамін (ч)	[wita'min]	vitamin
вода (ж)	[wo'da]	water
вуглеводи (ч)	[wuɦlɛ'wɔdɨ]	carbohydrates
вугор (ч)	[wu'ɦɔr]	eel
газований	[ɦa'zɔwanɨj]	carbonated
гамбургер (ч)	['ɦamburɦɛr]	hamburger
гарбуз (ч)	[ɦar'buz]	pumpkin
гарнір (ч)	[ɦar'nir]	side dish
гарячий	[ɦa'rʲatʃɨj]	hot
гвоздика (ж)	[ɦwoz'dɨka]	cloves
гіркий	[ɦir'kɨj]	bitter
гірчиця (ж)	[ɦir'tʃɨtsʲa]	mustard
горілка (ж)	[ɦo'rilka]	vodka
горіх (ч) волоський	[ɦo'rih wo'lɔsʲkɨj]	walnut
горіх (ч) кокосовий	[ɦo'rih ko'kɔsowɨj]	coconut
горох (ч)	[ɦo'rɔh]	pea
гранат (ч)	[ɦra'nat]	pomegranate
грейпфрут (ч)	[ɦrɛjp'frut]	grapefruit
гречка (ж)	['ɦrɛtʃka]	buckwheat
гриб (ч)	[ɦrib]	mushroom
груша (ж)	['ɦruʃa]	pear
гусак (ч)	[ɦu'sak]	goose
десерт (ч)	[dɛ'sɛrt]	dessert
джем (ч)	[dʒɛm]	jam
джин (ч)	[dʒin]	gin
диня (ж)	['dɨnʲa]	melon
дичина (ж)	[dɨtʃɨ'na]	game
дієта (ж)	[di'ɛta]	diet
жири (мн)	[ʒɨ'ri]	fats
жито (с)	['ʒɨto]	rye
жовток (ч)	[ʒow'tɔk]	egg yolk
жувальна гумка (ж)	[ʒu'walʲna 'ɦumka]	chewing gum
журавлина (ж)	[ʒuraw'lɨna]	cranberry
з газом	[z 'ɦazom]	sparkling
з льодом	[z lʲodom]	with ice
закуска (ж)	[za'kuska]	appetizer
заморожений	[zamo'rɔʒɛnɨj]	frozen
згущене молоко (с)	['zɦuɕɛnɛ molo'kɔ]	condensed milk
зелений чай (ч)	[zɛ'lɛnɨj tʃaj]	green tea
зелень (ж)	['zɛlɛnʲ]	greens
зерно (с)	[zɛr'nɔ]	grain
зернові рослини (мн)	[zɛrno'wi ros'lɨnɨ]	cereal crops
зморшок (ч)	['zmɔrʃok]	morel

зубочистка (ж)	[zubo'tʃistka]	toothpick
ікра (ж)	[ik'ra]	caviar
імбир (ч)	[im'bir]	ginger
індичка (ж)	[in'ditʃka]	turkey
інжир (ч)	[in'ʒir]	fig
їжа (ж)	['jiʒa]	food
їстівний гриб (ч)	[jis'tiwnij ɦrib]	edible mushroom
йогурт (ч)	['joɦurt]	yogurt
кабачок (ч)	[kaba'tʃɔk]	zucchini
кава (ж)	['kawa]	coffee
кава (ж) з вершками	['kawa z wɛrʃ'kami]	cappuccino
кава (ж) з молоком	['kawa z molo'kɔm]	coffee with milk
кавун (ч)	[ka'wun]	watermelon
калорія (ж)	[ka'lɔriʲa]	calorie
кальмар (ч)	[kalʲ'mar]	squid
камбала (ж)	[kamba'la]	flatfish
канапка (ж)	[ka'napka]	sandwich
капуста (ж)	[ka'pusta]	cabbage
капуста броколі (ж)	[ka'pusta 'brɔkoli]	broccoli
карта (ж) вин	['karta win]	wine list
картопля (ж)	[kar'tɔplʲa]	potato
картопляне пюре (с)	[kartop'lʲanɛ pʲu'rɛ]	mashed potatoes
качка (ж)	['katʃka]	duck
каша (ж)	['kaʃa]	porridge
квасоля (ж)	[kwa'sɔlʲa]	kidney bean
келих (ч)	['kɛlih]	glass
ківі (ч)	['kiwi]	kiwi
кмин (ч)	['kmin]	caraway
ковбаса (ж)	[kowba'sa]	sausage
коктейль (ч)	[kok'tɛjlʲ]	cocktail
колос (ч)	['kɔlos]	ear
кольорова капуста (ж)	[kolʲo'rɔwa ka'pusta]	cauliflower
кондитерські вироби (мн)	[kon'ditɛrsʲki 'wirobi]	confectionery
консерви (мн)	[kon'sɛrwi]	canned food
коньяк (ч)	[ko'nʲak]	cognac
копчений	[kop'tʃɛnij]	smoked
кориця (ж)	[ko'ritsʲa]	cinnamon
коріандр (ч)	[kori'andr]	coriander
короп (ч)	['kɔrop]	carp
краб (ч)	[krab]	crab
креветка (ж)	[krɛ'wɛtka]	shrimp
крем (ч)	[krɛm]	buttercream
крихта (ж)	['krihta]	crumb
кріль (ч)	[krilʲ]	rabbit
кріп (ч)	[krip]	dill
крупа (ж)	[kru'pa]	cereal grains
кукурудза (ж)	[kuku'rudza]	corn
кукурудза (ж)	[kuku'rudza]	corn
кукурудзяні пластівці (мн)	[kuku'rudzʲani plastiw'tsi]	cornflakes
кунжут (ч)	[kun'ʒut]	sesame

курка (ж)	['kurka]	chicken
кухня (ж)	['kuhnʲa]	cuisine
лавровий лист (ч)	[law'rɔwij list]	bay leaf
лангуст (ч)	[lan'ɦust]	spiny lobster
лимон (ч)	[li'mɔn]	lemon
лимонад (ч)	[limo'nad]	lemonade
лисичка (ж)	[li'sitʃka]	chanterelle
лід (ч)	[lid]	ice
лікер (ч)	[li'kɛr]	liqueur
ліщина (ж)	[li'ɕina]	hazelnut
ложка (ж)	['lɔʒka]	spoon
локшина (ж)	[lokʃi'na]	noodles
лосось (ч)	[lo'sɔsʲ]	salmon
лящ (ч)	[lʲaɕ]	bream
м'ясо (с)	['mʲ]aso]	meat
майонез (ч)	[maʲo'nɛz]	mayonnaise
макарони (мн)	[maka'rɔni]	pasta
малина (ж)	[ma'lina]	raspberry
манго (с)	['manɦo]	mango
мандарин (ч)	[manda'rin]	mandarin
маргарин (ч)	[marɦa'rin]	margarine
маринований	[mari'nɔwanij]	pickled
мармелад (ч)	[marmɛ'lad]	marmalade
мед (ч)	[mɛd]	honey
меню (с)	[mɛ'nʲu]	menu
мигдаль (ч)	[miɦ'dalʲ]	almond
мінеральна вода (ж)	[minɛ'ralʲna wo'da]	mineral water
молоко (с)	[molo'kɔ]	milk
молочний коктейль (ч)	[mo'lɔtʃnij kok'tɛjlʲ]	milkshake
морепродукти (мн)	[morɛpro'dukti]	seafood
морква (ж)	['mɔrkwa]	carrot
морозиво (с)	[mo'rɔziwo]	ice-cream
мухомор (ч)	[muho'mɔr]	fly agaric
начинка (ж)	[na'tʃinka]	filling
ніж (ч)	[niʒ]	knife
обід (ч)	[o'bid]	lunch
овес (ч)	[o'wɛs]	oats
овочі (мн)	['ɔwotʃi]	vegetables
огірок (ч)	[oɦi'rɔk]	cucumber
ожина (ж)	[o'ʒina]	blackberry
окіст (ч)	['ɔkist]	gammon
окунь (ч)	['ɔkunʲ]	perch
оливки (мн)	[o'liwki]	olives
олія (ж) оливкова	[o'liʲa o'liwkowa]	olive oil
олія (ж) рослинна	[o'liʲa ros'lina]	vegetable oil
омлет (ч)	[om'lɛt]	omelet
оселедець (ч)	[osɛ'lɛdɛts]	herring
осетрина (ж)	[osɛt'rina]	sturgeon
отруйний гриб (ч)	[ot'rujnij ɦrib]	poisonous mushroom
офіціант (ч)	[ofitsi'ant]	waiter
офіціантка (ж)	[ofitsi'antka]	waitress
оцет (ч)	['ɔtsɛt]	vinegar

палтус (ч)	['paltus]	halibut
папайя (ж)	[pa'paʲa]	papaya
паприка (ж)	['paprika]	paprika
паштет (ч)	[paʃ'tɛt]	pâté
перець (ч)	['pɛrɛts]	bell pepper
персик (ч)	['pɛrsik]	peach
петрушка (ж)	[pɛt'ruʃka]	parsley
печиво (с)	['pɛtʃiwo]	cookies
печінка (ж)	[pɛ'tʃinka]	liver
пиво (с)	['piwo]	beer
пиріг (ч)	[pi'rih]	pie
питна вода (ж)	[pit'na wo'da]	drinking water
підберезник (ч)	[pidbɛ'rɛznik]	birch bolete
підосичник (ч)	[pido'sitʃnik]	orange-cap boletus
піца (ж)	['pitsa]	pizza
поганка (ж)	[po'hanka]	death cap
полуниця (ж)	[polu'nitsʲa]	strawberry
помідор (ч)	[pomi'dɔr]	tomato
порічки (мн)	[po'ritʃki]	redcurrant
порція (ж)	['portsiʲa]	portion
приправа (ж)	[prip'rawa]	condiment
присмак (ч)	['prismak]	aftertaste
просо (с)	['prɔso]	millet
прохолодній напій (ч)	[proho'lɔdnij na'pij]	refreshing drink
прянощі (мн)	[prʲa'nɔɕi]	spice
пшениця (ж)	[pʃɛ'nitsʲa]	wheat
рахунок (ч)	[ra'hunok]	check
редька (ж)	['rɛdʲka]	radish
рецепт (ч)	[rɛ'tsɛpt]	recipe
риба (ж)	['riba]	fish
рис (ч)	[ris]	rice
ріпа (ж)	['ripa]	turnip
родзинки (мн)	[ro'dzinki]	raisin
розчинна кава (ж)	[roz'tʃina 'kawa]	instant coffee
ром (ч)	[rom]	rum
салат (ч)	[sa'lat]	lettuce
салат (ч)	[sa'lat]	salad
сардина (ж)	[sar'dina]	sardine
свинина (ж)	[swi'nina]	pork
свіжовижатий сік (ч)	[swiʒo'wiʒatij sik]	freshly squeezed juice
світле пиво (с)	['switlɛ 'piwo]	light beer
селера (ж)	[sɛ'lɛra]	celery
сир (ч)	[sir]	cheese
сироїжка (ж)	[siro'jiʒka]	russula
сік (ч)	[sik]	juice
сіль (ж)	[silʲ]	salt
скибка (ж)	['skibka]	slice
склянка (ж)	['sklʲanka]	glass
скумбрія (ж)	['skumbriʲa]	mackerel
слива (ж)	['sliwa]	plum
смажений	['smaʒɛnij]	fried
смак (ч)	[smak]	taste, flavor

смачний	[smatʃʲnij]	tasty
Смачного!	[smatʃʲnɔɦɔ]	Enjoy your meal!
сметана (ж)	[smɛˈtana]	sour cream
сніданок (ч)	[sniˈdanɔk]	breakfast
солодкий	[soˈlɔdkij]	sweet
солоний	[soˈlɔnij]	salty
сом (ч)	[som]	catfish
соняшникова олія (ж)	[ˈsɔnʲaʃnikowa oˈliʲa]	sunflower oil
сосиска (ж)	[soˈsɨska]	vienna sausage
соус (ч)	[ˈsous]	sauce
сочевиця (ж)	[sotʃɛˈwitsʲa]	lentil
соя (ж)	[ˈsɔʲa]	soy
спагеті (мн)	[spaˈɦɛti]	spaghetti
спаржа (ж)	[ˈsparʒa]	asparagus
столова ложка (ж)	[stoˈlɔwa ˈlɔʒka]	soup spoon
страва (ж)	[ˈstrawa]	course, dish
судак (ч)	[suˈdak]	pike perch
суниця (ж)	[suˈnitsʲa]	wild strawberry
сушений	[ˈsuʃɛnij]	dried
сьомга (ж)	[ˈsʲomɦa]	Atlantic salmon
тарілка (ж)	[taˈrilka]	plate
телятина (ж)	[tɛˈlʲatina]	veal
темне пиво (с)	[ˈtɛmnɛ ˈpiwo]	dark beer
тістечко (с)	[ˈtistɛtʃko]	cake
томатний сік (ч)	[toˈmatnij ˈsik]	tomato juice
торт (ч)	[tort]	cake
тріска (ж)	[trisˈka]	cod
тунець (ч)	[tuˈnɛts]	tuna
устриця (ж)	[ˈustritsʲa]	oyster
фарш (ч)	[farʃ]	hamburger
фінік (ч)	[ˈfinik]	date
фісташки (мн)	[fisˈtaʃki]	pistachios
форель (ж)	[foˈrɛlʲ]	trout
фрукт (ч)	[frukt]	fruit
хліб (ч)	[hlib]	bread
холодний	[hoˈlɔdnij]	cold
хрін (ч)	[hrin]	horseradish
цибуля (ж)	[tsiˈbulʲa]	onion
цукерка (ж)	[tsuˈkɛrka]	candy
цукор (ч)	[ˈtsukor]	sugar
чай (ч)	[tʃaj]	tea
чайна ложка (ж)	[ˈtʃajna ˈlɔʒka]	teaspoon
чайові (мн)	[tʃaʲoˈwi]	tip
часник (ч)	[tʃasˈnik]	garlic
чашка (ж)	[ˈtʃaʃka]	cup
червоне вино (с)	[tʃɛrˈwɔnɛ wiˈnɔ]	red wine
червоний перець (ч)	[tʃɛrˈwɔnij ˈpɛrɛts]	red pepper
черешня (ж)	[tʃɛˈrɛʃnʲa]	sweet cherry
чорна кава (ж)	[ˈtʃɔrna ˈkawa]	black coffee
чорна смородина (ж)	[ˈtʃɔrna smoˈrɔdina]	blackcurrant
чорний перець (ч)	[ˈtʃɔrnij ˈpɛrɛts]	black pepper
чорний чай (ч)	[ˈtʃɔrnij tʃaj]	black tea

чорниця (ж)	[tʃorˈnitsʲa]	bilberry
шампанське (с)	[ʃamˈpansʲkɛ]	champagne
шафран (ч)	[ʃafˈran]	saffron
шинка (ж)	[ˈʃinka]	ham
шкірка (ж)	[ˈʃkirka]	peel
шматок (ч)	[ʃmaˈtɔk]	piece
шоколад (ч)	[ʃokoˈlad]	chocolate
шоколадний	[ʃokoˈladnij]	chocolate
шпинат (ч)	[ʃpiˈnat]	spinach
штопор (ч)	[ˈʃtɔpor]	corkscrew
щука (ж)	[ˈɕuka]	pike
юшка (ж)	[ˈʲuʃka]	soup
яблуко (с)	[ˈʲabluko]	apple
ягода (ж)	[ˈʲaɦoda]	berry
ягоди (мн)	[ˈʲaɦodi]	berries
яєчня (ж)	[jaˈɛʃnʲa]	fried eggs
язик (ч)	[jaˈzik]	tongue
яйце (с)	[jajˈtsɛ]	egg
яйця (мн)	[ˈʲajtsʲa]	eggs
яловичина (ж)	[ˈʲalowitʃina]	beef
ячмінь (ч)	[jatʃˈminʲ]	barley

Printed in Great Britain
by Amazon